Praise for *FairPay*

Anyone responsible for monetizing digital content in consumer markets should understand this radically new perspective on pricing and how to maximize customer lifetime value. FairPay provides strategies and operational methods for creating better relationships—to increase loyalty, market reach, and profits.

—Shelly Palmer, Business Advisor, Author, Commentator

Reisman unveils a new world of possibilities through an innovative and visionary methodology that introduces a reference platform for digital value exchange. FairPay is very versatile in its applications and compatible across industries. It is a great example of what disruption could look like in a new digital business era.

—Lucila Pagnoni, News Corp Australia

FairPay boldly explores the future of pricing from a co-creation of value perspective. Highly recommended for digital business entrepreneurs, as well as established firms working on their digital transformation.

—Jim Spohrer, IBM and ISSIP.org

A groundbreaking and definitive book on pricing strategy for the digital age. This highly innovative and practical work shows how enterprises can develop relationship-based pricing strategies leading to long-term customer relationships, based on principles of equity and fairness for both customer and supplier.

—Professor Pennie Frow, University of Sydney Business School

FairPay

Adaptively Win–Win Customer Relationships

Richard Reisman

Foreword by Adrian Payne

BEP BUSINESS EXPERT PRESS

FairPay: Adaptively Win–Win Customer Relationships

First published in 2016 by
Business Expert Press, LLC
222 East 46th Street, New York, NY 10017
www.businessexpertpress.com

ISBN-13: 978-1-63157-477-1 (paperback)
ISBN-13: 978-1-63157-478-8 (e-book)

Business Expert Press Service Systems and Innovations in Business and Society Collection

Collection ISSN: 2326-2664 (print)
Collection ISSN: 2326-2699 (electronic)

Cover and interior design by Exeter Premedia Services Private Ltd., Chennai, India

First edition: 2016

10 9 8 7 6 5 4 3 2 1

Printed in the United States of America.

Abstract

Businesses everywhere are recognizing the need to be more customer-focused, but struggle to see how. At the same time, our logic and business models for selling digital content and services are recognized as broken. Digital relationships enable services at low cost, but we still focus on discrete transactions in which prices and value propositions are set by sellers in ways that customers often see as exploitive.

This book explains how a revolutionary new approach to pricing can solve these problems. It proposes a new architecture for cooperative service relationships that is personalized and continuously adaptive. FairPay operationalizes a *new logic* for conducting *ongoing business relationships* that *adaptively seek win–win value propositions* in which *price reflects value.*

At a practical level, this book explains how this new relationship architecture applies to a range of industries.

- A variety of business use cases are described, with motivations, and guidelines for process implementation in incremental stages. These are primarily for B2C digital content and services, including journalism, music, TV/video, books, games, software apps, and information services—but also for real services.
- Problems with current best practices are explained—including freemium and paywalls, all-you-can-eat subscriptions, and seller-set prices—and how the dynamically managed participative pricing of FairPay can enable far better price discrimination.

This has great promise to transform business by enhancing customer relationships, loyalty, market share, and profits.

At a conceptual level, this book suggests an "invisible handshake" in the form of participative "co-pricing" that dynamically seeks agreement on win–win value propositions.

- It seeks to approximate an ideal, perfectly discriminating price that is based on the actual value-in-context, as derived by individual customers during each of a series of transaction cycles—to enable a fair sharing of the value surplus between provider and customer.

- It applies modern behavioral economics in choice architectures that are implemented using computer-mediated dialogs—to enable deep relationship marketing, and lead to a bottom line accounting that tracks to holistic metrics of value.

Keywords

behavioral economics, business models, co-creation, co-pricing, customer journeys, customer relationships, digital content, digital media, digital services, FairPay, freemium, microeconomics, participative pricing, paywalls, pay what you want, price discrimination, pricing strategy, relationship marketing, reputation, subscriptions, value propositions

Contents

Foreword by Adrian Payne

Enterprises everywhere are recognizing the need to become more customer-focused, but struggle to determine how to achieve this. This compelling book explains how a new innovative approach to pricing—"FairPay"—can help achieve this goal through a radical shift in considering how to price products and services. Pricing is not an area that executives consider with great excitement, yet the approach outlined by Richard Reisman promises to be transformative both in practice and theory. It is likely to receive great interest from enterprises, especially those offering digital products and services where the marginal cost of producing a further unit is close to zero.

Today it is common, for most suppliers, to set a price and then for consumers to either accept or reject the offer. This has not always been the case as, until the mid-19th century, negotiation and bargaining were the main means of arriving at a price for most purchases. However, with the advent of retailing and retail stores, fixed prices largely replaced negotiating and bargaining practices. Although the advent of fixed pricing greatly simplified transactions and improved operational efficiency, it left little room for flexibility and the recognition that different customer segments, and different individual customers, are willing to pay different prices based on the perceived value of the product or service being offered to them.

Today, customers in all industries are shifting from being passive participants to active collaborators. This represents substantial opportunities to improve customer focus and address the enterprise's key tasks of winning, keeping, and growing customers. The ideas in this book resonate strongly with me as a result of my long-term research work in relationship marketing and customer relationship management (CRM). This book offers a new strategy for operationalizing a participative form of pricing that promises to drive deep adoption and bottom line impact, especially in our new digital world. It embodies the lessons of recent decades of conceptual advances in relationship marketing, CRM, customer retention, pricing strategy, customer experience, co-creation of value, and value proposition design. The book provides a new logic—a new operational dynamic for maximizing customer lifetime value based on direct learning about what different customers value longitudinally over time.

This carefully researched work builds on recent behavioral economics research and business experience on participative pricing and shows how new pricing strategies can be used to achieve sustainable profitability in mass consumer markets. In the last decade in particular many consumer markets such as newspapers, music, and, increasingly, video are facing desperate straits. Traditional pricing models for such industries are becoming outdated as they do not reflect customers' dynamic perceptions of value. The ideas in this book represent a new approach that can help enterprises maximize their most important asset—the lifetime value of their base of customers. This approach has the greatest likely utility for digital products, yet both digital and conventional markets can be expected to benefit from value propositions that seek to provide greater equity and fairness to customers.

Over the last decade there have been a number of developments in developing more flexible pricing approaches, including "pay what you want," "freemium," and others. The "FairPay" model takes participative pricing to a new level, where customers can experience and use the product or service offer before payment. As a result they are then in a much better position to determine a fair price based on their individual sense of value. This potentially represents a much more equitable distribution of value for both customer and supplier. Critically it provides a new basis for segmenting customers based on price, which permits a much more granular understanding of the different levels of value experienced by different customers. The approach outlined in this book enables suppliers to develop more focused and flexible value propositions that reflect the customer's real willingness to pay. Customer involvement in pricing in this way can offer opportunities for enhancing relationships, building trust and an increase in fairness and commitment to one-another, with resulting increase in long-term customer value.

The "FairPay" model capitalises on the nature of digital services (and other experience goods/services) and can permit the power of computer-mediated, data-driven customer journeys to be unleashed through adapting value propositions to individual contexts over a relationship, working through new dynamic feedback/control processes. Importantly, it can co-exist with conventional methods but it can gradually displace them in those markets and segments where that is most advantageous. Most critically, by introducing the concept of the "long tail of customers" it shows how enterprises can benefit from those customers who are willing to pay more than the set price—as well as those customers who are not willing to pay the set price, but are willing to pay some reasonable price above the marginal cost. It has great potential to exploit automation, "big data," predictive analytics, and advanced CRM, yet can be initiated with simple rules-based processing.

The author, Richard Reisman, is the president and founder of Tele-shuttle Corporation. He is a highly regarded entrepreneur and inventor in digital content industries. Billions of users have benefited from his prior inventions. The "FairPay" pricing model, his most recent inno-vation, represents a bold new opportunity for companies to break the legacy bonds of "fixed pricing" and build customer relationships and long-term customer value through a more equitable form of engagement. This important new framework for equity-based pricing is worthy of strong consideration by businesses wishing to develop a deeper customer focus. It has great promise for enterprises wishing to transform business by enhancing customer relationships, loyalty, market share, and profits. Businesses and entrepreneurs should think about how to test and build on this innovation and gain the benefits of a first mover advantage.

Adrian Payne
Professor of Marketing
University of New South Wales Business School, Australia
Visiting Professor, Cranfield School of Management
Cranfield University, UK

Preface

FairPay has become my mission. I have always been a bit of a techno-utopian—but pragmatic and human-centered. From my first summer job at Bell Labs, my interest in information and communications technology has been focused on how it can make life better for people. That gained focus around 1970 from the work of Nelson, Engelbart, Licklider, and others on "man-machine symbiosis," "augmenting human intellect," and hypermedia. After a varied career at the leading edge of media technology, seeing many of the visions that drive me becoming commonplace (but many still elusive), I came to the vision of FairPay. From that perspective, I saw that the most fundamental crisis in media that I can hope to influence is not what it is (developing nicely for the most part), but how people buy it and sustain its production (badly stuck).

Our logic and business models for buying and selling digital content and services are broken. We see general directions for change, but no clear mechanisms for moving that from high-level "motherhood" and tacked-on ideals into nitty-gritty business processes that drive behavior. FairPay offers a process that is simple, and promises to be practical. This is not limited to digital, but points toward a more win–win economics across the board.

My focus has been on markets as an emergent process for optimizing value for people. FairPay is an architecture that itself embodies an emergent process of value-centered testing and adaptation. It applies proven principles in a new combination that will be shaped to specific business environments. It will continually evolve and improve in response to learning about (and shaping) customer behaviors.

This book is a call to action—to get more people to see the potential, and to help move FairPay from idea to commonplace reality.

A challenge in writing and reading this book is its dual focus: both the operational details of FairPay as structured to work in specific businesses, as well as the more conceptual aspects of how it enables a new economics. I sought to separate those two tracks. Portions can be skipped, but

I hope most readers will find this dual vision adds understanding and motivation.

This book addresses a wide range of business issues in a variety of industries, plus a theoretical base spanning marketing, economics, psychology, and game theory. I am hardly an expert in those domains, and any errors are mine alone. My hope is that any errors are in fine points, and that domain experts will see the bigger picture and find it compelling.

Online Supplement—FPZLink—at FPZLink.com

An online supplement to this book provides more background and examples, links to references, as well as updates.

Acknowledgments

This work draws on a lifetime of learning, "standing on the shoulders of giants," as well as thought-provoking discussions about FairPay with hundreds of very smart people in business and academia. Apologies for any omissions from this partial list of influential contributors.

My earliest significant scholarly collaboration on FairPay has been with Marco Bertini (thanks to Dan Ariely and Ayelet Gneezy for that introduction). Next has been with Adrian Payne and Pennie Frow (who together introduced me to Jim Spohrer). Special thanks to Adrian for his very helpful suggestions on this manuscript. Thanks to Jim Spohrer for requesting that I write this book and helping to shape it, and to Haluk Demirkan and others at ISSIP, and the very supportive team at BEP, that helped make it a reality. And thanks to the many other scholars who have contributed to these ideas.

On the business side, special thanks for very helpful support of these ideas and how to develop them from my colleagues Robert Gordon, Robert Westerlund, Craig Mowry, Alex Cohen, Richard Jagacinski, Bryan Finkel, Steve Sieck, Bill Rosenblatt, James Monaco, Jerrold Spiegel, Ben Boissevain, Jeff Einstein, Yiannis Kourakis, Eleanor Haas, Lori Hoberman, Katja Bartholmess, and Shelly Palmer, and from John Blossom (Shore Communications), Brendan Benzing (Rhapsody), Jim Schachter (New York Times), Frank Ernst (Zuora), Steve Outing (Digital News Test Kitchen), TJ Vitolo (Verizon), Peter Scheuch (Ennovent), Aleks Jakulin (Ganxy), Paul Zagaeski (GigaOM), Jeremy Billy (Gannett), Lucila Pagnoni (News Corp), Maryam Ashfar (MECLABS), Trevor Kaufman (Tinypass/Piano), Lily Varon (Forrester), Ron Huddleston (Salesforce), Benji Roberts (PledgeMusic), as well as many others.

And special thanks to my wonderful wife Dana Reed for her unwavering support.

Prolog: A Thought Experiment—Imagine a Value-Pricing Demon …

Imagine a demon that might power a system of commerce. Imagine that this demon has perfect ability to observe activity and read the minds of buyers and sellers to determine individualized "value-in-use"—the actual value perceived and realized by each buyer, at each stage of using a product or service.

- *The demon knows how each buyer uses the product or service, how much they like it, what value it provides them, and how that relates to their larger objectives and willingness/ability to pay. It understands the ever-changing attributes of current context, where the value of a given item or unit of service can depend on when and how it is experienced.*
- *Furthermore, this demon can determine the* economic value surplus *of the offering—how much value it generates beyond the cost to produce and deliver it.*
- *The demon can go even farther, to act as an arbiter of how the economic surplus can be shared fairly between the producer and the customer. How much of the surplus should go to the customer, as a value gain over the price paid, and how much should go the producer, as a profit over the cost of production and delivery, to sustain their ability to continue those activities.*

Such a commerce demon might thus serve as the brains of a system that sets prices that are adaptive and personalized—to set a price for each person, at each time, that is fair to both the producer and the customer. Imagine we could build an e-commerce system, with advanced programming and data that worked as an artificial intelligence version of this demon. Prices would not be pre-set by the seller, but would be set dynamically by the demon for each item or unit of service, at levels that would be fair and acceptable to both the buyer and seller.

Actually, a rather different pricing demon has long been widely accepted as central to our economics. Isn't Adam Smith's invisible hand just the hand of a demon that guides the setting of prices based on a balance of supply and demand?

So if we have Adam Smith's demon, why do we need my demon? Because the invisible hand works nicely for markets of scarcity, but in the digital era, we face markets of abundance. The task of these new markets is not how to allocate scarce goods, but how to sustain the creation of services that can be replicated without cost or limit. What we now need to allocate is a fair share of the customer's wallet.

This book shows how thinking about my demon can help us do that. *FairPay is a business architecture centered on a new value feedback process that adaptively seeks to approximate what the demon knows.*

(More on thought experiments and this demon in Chapter 5.)

PART I

The Big Picture—A New Logic

CHAPTER 1

Introduction—Digital Disruption and Yesterday's Logic

The greatest danger in times of turbulence is not the turbulence, it is to act with yesterday's logic.

—Peter Drucker

FairPay is a *new logic* for conducting *ongoing business relationships* that *adaptively seek win–win value propositions* in which *price reflects value*.

FairPay is a logic for seeking to learn and apply what my pricing demon knows (see Prolog). It is an architecture for business processes that are adaptively configured to seek win–win with customers cooperatively, in a new kind of equity-based dynamic pricing.

The idea for FairPay arose in response to the new challenges (and opportunities) of selling digital services in networked markets, and may be most applicable there—at least initially. But there is reason to think that it will work well for some physical product/service businesses, and in time might be useful far more broadly. Much of this book focuses on digital services, but the wider potential is outlined as well.

We all recognize that we are at the infancy of a digital era, with the mantra that "the Internet changes everything." Our society, business, markets, media, services, and even our most basic human communications and relationships are mediated by digital communications networks and computer processing. We have recognized the need for new logic in many aspects of business in this strange new world, but the most central aspect of our markets, the setting of price, has barely changed at all. Our core approach to how customers and service providers relate to one another needs a radically new logic that addresses the new realities of *digital services* in *networked markets*.

We are facing huge turbulence in these markets, most visible in content industries that have been disrupted by digital, so that the very nature of how we think of value has come loose. Major industries such as music and newspapers are being devastated, with others such as TV/video/movies beginning to see disruption. Long-established businesses are in turmoil, and even nimble upstarts have challenges in making their value propositions attractive beyond narrow markets. It is hard to get consumers to be willing to pay, and the traditional alternative of advertising support is increasingly threatened. Companies face threats of piracy and bypass (via Google and Facebook). Advertising is under siege by technical challenges (including the shift to mobile) and growing consumer rebellion in the form of ad-blocking.

Our consumer value propositions are just not working well. Too many consumers are just not willing to pay the prices that companies think they should. Many companies fed into that by offering digital content services free, and now find it problematic to charge.

There are a number of fundamental reasons why traditional methods do not work for pricing digital experiences in networked markets:

- *Replication is nearly free*—The invisible hand flails aimlessly, having no scarcity of supply to ration against demand— pricing becomes an arbitrary shot at what "the market" will bear. Meanwhile many consumers think that "information wants to be free" and question why they should pay at all.
- *Value is experiential, personal, and context-dependent*— Conventional pre-setting of prices by producers fails to relate to wide variations in value received. There is not one market, but a multitude of markets of one, each of which fluctuates over time.
- *Relationships are the new marketing*—Conventional efforts at "relationship marketing" have been bolted on to traditional transaction-oriented business practices and only scratch the surface of true relationships that seek to maximize customer lifetime value (CLV). Companies are beginning to recognize

the importance of "customer journeys" and "loyalty loops" but are just beginning to understand how to integrate them into business practices.

Recognizing the importance of these factors, freemium subscription models have emerged as the current best practice in many industries. Freemium (*free* + pre*mium*) is a step toward relationship-building in which a limited level of free service is used as a loss-leader to attract as many potential users as possible, with the hope of then converting them to a premium level that they can be convinced to pay for once they have experienced at least some of the value. But freemium is just one limited step in the right direction. It fails to exploit networked relationships to seek pricing that customers can see as fair.

Digital businesses face two fundamental problems:

1. *The driving problem is how to make the business sustainably profitable in this digital era.*
2. *That problem centers on difficult questions of price—free or paid? and how set?*

A New Logic

FairPay is a simple but fundamental rethinking of how businesses and consumers conduct exchanges with one another in a digital marketplace.

- It proposes a new architecture for approximating an optimal price—one that is personal and dynamically context-dependent—by building a deep relationship that is based on dialogs about value.
- It embodies modern concepts of business as the co-creation of value by businesses and customers working cooperatively.
- It provides a new and empowering process for co-pricing, a form of participative pricing.

FairPay makes dialogs about value a central feature of a new kind of emergent learning relationship that becomes an integral focus of each customer journey—to shape what people are offered, what they buy, and at what price. It moves from the mass-market tyranny of set-pricing, to person-alized, dynamic pricing—in a way that uniquely develops trust, fairness, loyalty, and profit—to maximize CLV for as many customers as can be served profitably—and can factor in social values as well.

- FairPay re-envisions elements of freemium; paywalls; sub-scriptions; membership or loyalty programs; dynamic pricing; value-/performance-/outcomes-based pricing; and pay what you want (PWYW), to provide a strong and sustainable customer relationship and revenue stream.
- FairPay solves the nasty problems of pricing digital products and other experience goods—by seeking to approach optimal price discrimination, based on in-depth learning about each customer—and does this in a relationship-centered, participa-tory way that assures customer buy-in.
- It is this relationship focus at the core of FairPay that creates a new dimension to B2C customer relationships—one that previously has only been approximated in high-end industrial B2B value-/performance-/outcomes-based pricing.
- FairPay builds on the lessons of PWYW participative pric-ing, in consumer markets—but adds this new dimension of feedback and control over ongoing relationships to make that more sustainably profitable.

The core process enabling FairPay works over relationships, by applying a deceptively simple balance of powers:

1. *Selectively empower the buyer to unilaterally set whatever value-based price the buyer considers fair—after the sale, when the real value is expe-rienced and known.*
2. *Track that buyer value-based price and determine whether the seller agrees that is fair, and use that information to empower the seller to decide whether to make further offers on those terms to that buyer in the future. (Unfair buyers are eventually downgraded to lesser offers or fixed-price.)*
3. *Continue this balancing in future transactions, to build a relationship based on fair value exchange that adapts and evolves over time, frames*

the value that was delivered, and a suggested price for that—and nudges the buyer to be generous by offering more value in the future for more generosity now.

This repeating cycle gives buyers a strong incentive to price fairly, to build a beneficial relationship—and enables sellers to limit their future exposure to those who do not—using decision rules that can readily be tuned to specific situations, segments, and objectives (see Figure 1.1).

At first glance, this core process may appear to have limited effectiveness and applicability, but on closer scrutiny it can be viewed as representing a profound shift—*shifting the entire focus on customer relationships from price to value.* As such it has the potential to transform how companies manage customer relationships, integrating a new dimension—of time and relationship—that has previously only been tacked on to transaction-oriented exchanges. This book explains how and why this is workable.

Many have seen potential in participatory pricing, but seller control and predictability has been a big concern—how can the powers of buyer and seller be fairly balanced to lead to sustainably win–win pricing? FairPay makes participatory co-pricing practical, controllable, and profitable

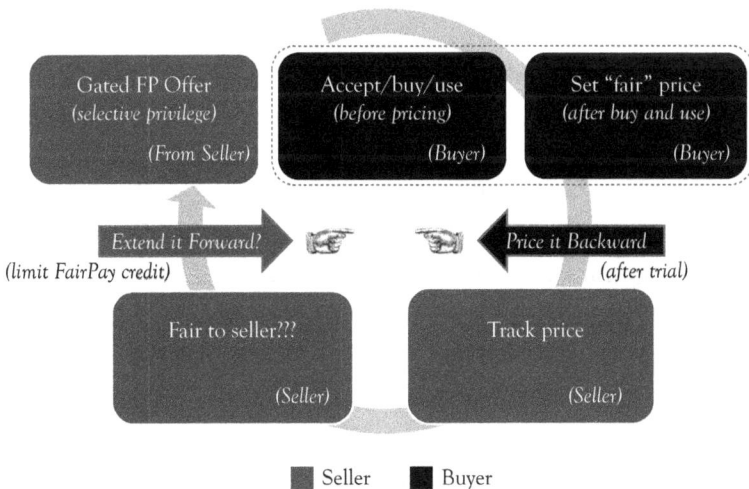

Figure 1.1 FairPay participative process

Source: www.fairpayzone.com/2011/03/fairpay-pricing-some-process-diagrams.html

for mainstream consumer business use. It does this by turning it into a repeated game—using structured dialogs (choice architectures) plus Internet-enabled tracking, to limit price-setting privileges to only those who price fairly over an ongoing relationship, and to guide customers to price fairly. These dialogs generate a whole new level of customer feedback on their experiences—and their real willingness to pay for them—as that evolves over the relationship.

I first outlined FairPay in 2010 on my blog at FairPayZone.com. This book draws heavily on the materials in that blog (see FPZLink). A brief introduction coauthored with Marco Bertini was published in the Harvard Business Review blog series in 2013 (Bertini and Reisman 2013) and a further paper is pending publication (Reisman and Bertini 2014). Other collaborations with Adrian Payne and Pennie Frow led to a presentation at the Naples Forum on Service in 2015 (Frow, Reisman, and Payne 2015), and further collaborative work is in progress.

How It Works—Customer Participation in Pricing as a Privilege

We have been conditioned to think only of seller-set prices (the price tag) or traditional negotiation (haggling over price) that work in a context of isolated transactions. *FairPay is a logic that operates more holistically—it introduces a new kind of balance of powers that works over a series of transactions to build a relationship.* A customer is selectively granted new power to set prices, but the seller decides whether to continue granting that power to that customer. The relationship continues as long as both are satisfied. This feedback control loop creates a new logic for adaptively seeking win–win value that grounds and enriches the customer journey.

It is anticipated that FairPay would be *offered to customers selectively, as a privilege, as an alternative to a conventional pricing* such as a paywall, but that conventional set-price paywalls would remain for customers who do not adapt well to this new responsibility for fair, win–win pricing—the implicit contract of what I call an "invisible handshake" (as explained later).

FairPay is designed to become a primary pricing model, but first it can be trialed in low-risk tests, such as premium tiers and loyalty programs, customer acquisition/retention, or for other selected product tiers or market segments. It builds stronger customer relationships for greater profit from a wider market. Early uses should be targeted to customer segments expected to take well to it—starting with the most promising relationships—and then gradually expand more broadly as its benefits become clear, and customers become familiar with this new logic.

The core mechanism suggested for FairPay is outlined in the following boxes and Figure 1.1.

How FairPay Works

... over a relationship,

... through a deceptively simple balancing dynamic:

1. Selectively empower the buyer to unilaterally set whatever value-based price the buyer considers fair—*after the sale, when the real value is experienced and known.*

2. Track that buyer value-based price and determine whether the seller agrees that is fair, and use that information to empower the seller to decide whether to make further offers *on those terms to that buyer in the future.* (Unfair buyers are eventually downgraded to lesser offers or fixed price.)

3. *Continue this balancing in future transactions,* to build a relationship based on fair value exchange, which adapts and evolves over time. Frame the value that was delivered, and a suggested price for that—and nudge the buyer to be generous by offering more value for more generosity.

This revocable privilege gives buyers a strong incentive to price fairly—and enables sellers to limit their future exposure to those who do not.

More broadly, it shifts the entire focus of customer relationships from price to value.

Consumers—Pay only what seems fair to you:

- *Pay what you think fair* for products or services—*after you try them.*
- Make every purchase on a trial basis—so you can always *be sure to get your personal fair value* for your money.
- *Agree to set your price fairly—in your judgment—and explain why you think it is fair.*
- *Maintain that privilege as long as you can convince the seller that you are being fair.*

Businesses—Get the most revenue from the most customers by continuously learning what each one values:

- Engage in *real dialog with each of your customers* and listen to their perceptions of the value they get from your products/services.
- Make a trial offer to *every potential customer* who sees potential value.
- Suggest a price after use that you think is fair for that particular customer, considering usage and all other relevant factors.
- Provide incentives, such as premium tiers and perks, to entice fairness, and even generosity.
- Let your customers *self-select into segments* (based on usage, value perception, willingness and ability to pay, …)
- *Limit your risk from those trial offers by tracking the results (fairness) for each buyer, and limiting future offers if you judge that buyer to not pay fairly.*
- Retain set-price plans for those who refuse to be fair.
- Learn how much freedom (FairPay credit) to extend (or what restrictions to enforce) to get satisfactory results from each customer segment.
- Continue to make every offer a trial, …

> • … as long as each buyer continues paying fairly (at least most of the time)—*in your judgment.*
>
> *Delight your customers*: Give them what they really want, at a price they really think fair.
>
> *Shift the conversation from price to value.*
>
> *Empower them* to engage with you and tell you what they value.

Keep in mind that, in its purest form, this process never sets final prices in advance of a transaction. It is not a way to negotiate transaction prices that then are pre-set going forward. That could be done, but then the whole dynamic of adaptation to value as it changes in context over time would be lost. At times it may be desirable to put this process on autopilot, to limit the frequency of pricing dialogs once a stable situation seems to exist—but to maintain the full power of FairPay, prices should always remain open to unilateral reset by the customer, based on their current experience.

Why It Works

Behavioral economics: FairPay builds on extensive behavioral economics research to shift from simple transactional behaviors to more collaborative behaviors:

- To give sellers control of how much power to yield to buyers, depending on how well they pay over an ongoing learning relationship;
- To segment buyers based on their payment behavior; and
- To nudge buyers to pay generously, using structured dialogs and incentives.

Many ask why customers would pay if they do not have to, but extensive experience with even simple, purely voluntary forms of PWYW pricing shows that *people actually do pay, even when they do not have to.*

People have an inherent desire to be fair. Understanding and applying these motivations is central to making FairPay work well, and we will explore this from many angles. And keep in mind that FairPay's conditional extension of offers adds controls to restrict customers who choose to price unfairly.

Game theory: Even the hard-headed *homo economicus*, the rational, self-interested utility maximizer of classical economics (not just the *homo reciprocans* of behavioral economics), will see the compelling logic of FairPay. FairPay is structured as a "repeated game" in which it is worthwhile to pay up, to invest in reputation building, in order to maximize FairPay access to future purchases. It is just a matter of careful and constantly adaptive game design to ensure that the game remains win–win (and that any losses from those who seek to game the system or to play unfairly and then quit are limited to be acceptably small).

Basic economics: It has long been known that the most economically efficient prices are not uniform, but are customized for each customer to the actual value they receive, and their willingness to pay for it. This is true in the theory of optimal price discrimination, and has been proven effective in high-end B2B businesses where actual value-in-use can be cooperatively evaluated and used to set prices based on performance and outcomes. Doing that in mass consumer markets had seemed unfeasible, but FairPay now points the way to doing just that, in a consumer-friendly way.

Customer journeys: Modern marketing practice is increasingly focused on fostering customer journeys that develop "loyalty loops" to maximize the repeat business that leads to sustainable profit. What better way to build strong loyalty loops than to center them on true dialogs about individual value perceptions?

Where It Works

- FairPay promises to be most useful for any product/service where low marginal costs apply, so a seller can afford to put a limited amount of product at risk in order to seek to build a profitable relationship with a customer. This includes most forms of digital content (newspapers, magazines, music, video, e-books, and games), software/apps, and services (of any kind) offered to consumers (or low-end B2B offers).

- It can also apply to perishing items of any kind, including physical products/services (much like Priceline and Groupon).

- Even for products/services for which there is a high variable cost, FairPay can be used with a seller-set minimum price floor that at least covers the variable cost, to focus on fair sharing of the rest of the value surplus. (The base price can be paid up front, while the value bonus can be set and paid after the experience is known.)

- FairPay is especially relevant to experience goods and services, where the perceived value depends on the usage by the particular customer, as they perceive it, in their unique usage context—which cannot be reliably predicted in advance. More and more, we are in such an "experience economy."

Businesses should begin by seeking low-hanging fruit. Initial sweet spots will be with customers who are disposed to high fairness and generosity—such as superfans getting much-appreciated service from deserving providers—and wherever the seller has a particularly strong human appeal to sustainable compensation, whether based on service quality or social contributions. Once the power of FairPay is demonstrated in such sweet spots (even if only with a minority of customers), broader expansion will become more and more compelling to both customers and firms.

In addition to better pricing, FairPay generates a new kind of detailed database on each customer's fairness and willingness to pay for specific value propositions—a new kind of Big Data about value, a Cloud of Value—that can become an essential tool for targeting marketing offers.

FairPay can be applied by individual content/service businesses, but it gains economies of scale and network effects when applied across a platform serving multiple provider/seller businesses. For platform providers, this database Cloud of Value can be leveraged across the platform to predict how known customers will respond to new providers—creating a valuable asset much like a credit rating database. Learning how fairly individual customers pay current providers enables predictions about how they will deal with new providers, so that this learning process can be leveraged across a whole market ecosystem. That can enable offers to be targeted to those who are most likely to respond cooperatively, even for new service providers.

How Do You Get FairPay?

FairPay is a logic, not a product—it is an architecture for a new way of doing business. I have been working on FairPay on a pro-bono basis (in collaboration with prominent marketing scholars).

- The concepts have been developed in depth and published, starting in 2010. The precursor elements of FairPay have all been proven in commercial use, but the full FairPay control process has not yet been put into use. FairPay has generated wide interest, and discussions on implementation and trials of the full process are underway.
- The expectation is that some individual businesses will implement FairPay services themselves, and some will rely on platform providers who will offer core FairPay software and services. There have been promising ongoing discussions with both selling businesses and platform providers.
- Proof of concept testing is needed to validate and refine our understanding of how consumers will respond to this conditional grant of pricing power, and how businesses can best manage the process to frame value propositions, nudge behaviors, and define decision rules that elicit sustainable pricing behavior.
- There are many variations in how FairPay can be applied. Even if initial tests fail to generate the desired results, they will provide insight into how to adapt these methods to work better. FairPay moves us toward a model that is consistent with leading-edge thinking in marketing. Starting down that path will almost certainly lead us to an approach that works far better than current methods.

CHAPTER 2

Business Overview—Part 1

Basic Concepts—How and Why

Price Should Reflect Value

We are so used to our current practices of seller-pre-set prices that discriminate poorly (yesterday's logic), that we tend to not realize how that distorts our economy and makes it inefficient—especially now that there are major sectors where scarcity of supply is simply a non-issue. Why do all users of a service—such as digital newspaper or digital music or video subscription service—pay the same price? Some use such services heavily, others lightly. Some obtain high value from the services, others just minimal levels of value. Some are affluent and some are not. Yet they all pay the same price.

The focus of this book is on why that is not simply a matter of being unfair, but how it makes markets inefficient, reduces demand, and results in a deadweight loss to our economy. Many pay less than they should—and many more forgo using such services at all because the price is too high, even though sales at a lower price acceptable to them would create added value and profit that would be a clear win–win.

The essential logic of FairPay is that *price should reflect value*—in context as used—and over time. An efficient economics must seek to approach that over each relationship. It is the logic of seeking to approximate and apply what my pricing demon knows about value.

Isn't that the only win–win way to do business? Why should we—both businesses and customers—settle for prices that do not reflect the best reasonable approximation of the actual value the customer receives? Of course, as we will explore, in setting prices that reflect value, we must also factor in the cost to the provider, and a fair sharing of the value surplus over that cost between the producer and the customer.

FairPay is a <u>new logic</u> for conducting <u>ongoing relationships</u> that <u>adaptively seek win–win value propositions</u> in which <u>price corresponds to value</u>.

- The core idea is that *prices should reflect value*. Not the producer's preconception of value for an average customer, but what value a particular customer actually perceives as realized in the experience of using the product or service, in the fullness of their individual context (the value my demon sees).

- Such a concept of price corresponding to value is *win–win for both the producer and the customer*. They agree to do business if they expect a value surplus over cost, and both benefit if they share that value surplus fairly—fair value to the customer, and a fair profit to sustain and motivate the producer. It allows a producer to provide value to a maximum number of customers who seek it, in a way that can maximize revenue and profit as well—especially for products and services (such as digital content) for which customers may challenge any pre-set price as arbitrary and unfairly out of line with their actual perceived value.

- *Adaptively seeking* such win–win value propositions is required because the valuation considerations are complex. It is hard to do this accurately for any one transaction (which is why value-based pricing is now done only in high-value B2B contexts). But an adaptive, intuitively reasonable approximation can be cooperatively converged upon over a series of transactions—and can continuously adjust as things change over time.

- *Ongoing relationships* provide an environment that justifies and enables the process of adaptively seeking those win–win value propositions. If the marginal costs of the product/ service are low, producers can afford to take limited risks at the start of a relationship (just as they do with free trials or freemium), in hopes of building a productive and loyal relationship that is profitable over the lifetime of the relationship. Both parties learn to see and compare notes on what my demon sees.

- *FairPay is a new logic* in that this idea—that price must be co-created, as a dynamic and personalized approximation of value as exchanged—creates a very different conceptual framework for how our markets work. It shifts us from a mentality of take-it-or-leave-it prices pre-set by producers, which are often unfair, to a cooperative process of creating value in a way that explicitly seeks to be fairly win–win.

From this perspective, FairPay is a form of co-pricing for services, in which buyer and seller agree on a process to adaptively seek a win–win value exchange—not focused just on single transactions, but over the life of their relationship. That ongoing relationship perspective opens up a whole new dimension in customer relationships that can deeply alter how we do business—transforming the nature of the customer journey, as well as the workings of our broader business ecosystems.

An All-knowing Economic Demon Informing an Invisible Handshake

So FairPay is a process, an engine for seeking to approximate what my demon knows—an economic demon that reads the minds of buyers and seller to determine the actual value-in-context for each transaction, figures out the value surplus (over cost), and negotiates an equitable sharing of that value surplus between the producer and customer.

Prices set by such a demon are win–win for both sides. The FairPay process of repeating dialogs about value over a series of transactions serves as a way to approximate what that demon knows, at least on average, over time.

This can be viewed as an "invisible handshake"—an agreement between the producer and customer to work together through the FairPay process to try to come to a common understanding of individual value propositions over time, and to co-design them. An agreement to cooperate—to seek transparency and honesty—to come to a joint understanding of value—so that we can jointly seek to maximize that value for the benefit of both of us. While this emergent approximation may not be very accurate for any one transaction (especially when the relationship is new), the process seeks to converge on a level of fairness over time, as the parties get to understand one another. This handshake is a repeated game—when properly structured, it is in both parties' interest to collaborate on seeking win–win. (This variation on Smith's invisible hand is expanded on in Chapter 5.)

FairPay is win–win for both producers and customers because it allows producers to sell to all customers who find value in the producer's service, at prices that are dynamically personalized to approximate ideal price discrimination. That leads to a near-maximum number of profitable and loyal relationships, to maximize total revenue and total value creation. It also enables a near-maximum number of risk-free trials by customers who think they might find value. All of this brings more value to more people.

Service Relationships—Win–Win Customer Journeys Based on Dialogs About Value

This cooperative focus on value ties in with a number of emerging trends in marketing strategy. FairPay fits well with these new concepts, and offers a way to make them more concrete, with results that flow directly to the bottom line. Consider the following trends, which can be seen as complementary perspectives on marketing, and on the new logic of FairPay:

- A pervasive new logic for marketing and business in general is the explicit focus of the emerging body of work on a "Service-Dominant Logic" (Lusch and Vargo 2014), in contrast to the "Goods-Dominant Logic" that developed over the past centuries—"yesterday's logic." Now we are in a service-dominant economy, and are beginning to realize that the value of goods is really in how they enable and help deliver a service. (My use of the Drucker quote and the idea of a logic builds on that work.) FairPay centers on the questions of how we set value on services. This is especially relevant to digital services (including content services and software), where replication is essentially free.
- A related emerging focus is the idea of "co-creation of value" (Payne and Frow 2013). This becomes especially clear when

we consider the logic of services, and look beyond our obsolete logic of goods. A significant body of work emphasizes that value is not just created by an active producer and handed over to a passive customer, but is actively co-created by the process in which they work together to realize a service, and to share in the value of the experience that the service creates. That leads to realization that there is a whole chain of collaborative activities such as co-design, coproduction, copromotion, co-pricing, codistribution, and the like. From this perspective, FairPay is an embodiment of co-pricing that seeks to fairly share in the value that is co-created.

- A third emerging focus is that of the "customer journey" (Edelman and Singer 2015). For most businesses it has become clear that the real objective of customer relationship management is not just to respond to problems, and to deal with isolated transactions, but to proactively focus on ongoing relationships, to seek to retain customers and maximize customer lifetime value (CLV). The idea of the customer journey is emerging as the way to close and tighten the "loyalty loop" on repeat sales. FairPay builds on that perspective by adding explicit dialogs about value into every cycle of the loyalty loop.

CHAPTER 3

Business Overview—Part 2

Rethinking Prices

So Last Century!—What Is a Price, and Why?

We think we know what a price is, but *a price has an economic function, and that function has changed.*

- Through most of history a price was the outcome of a personal negotiation between human buyers and sellers, depending on the needs and powers of each, in an individualized context of personal interaction and knowledge of one another. Different buyers got different prices. Prices were a very personal thing. Buyer and seller were usually part of a community, and communal norms encouraged social values of caring, and even generosity between buyers and sellers.

- Over the last century or so, institutionalized mass-marketing pushed that to the margins. Consumers no longer bought from individuals, but from institutions with standardized prices—starting with department stores in the mid-1800s. The relationship became asymmetric, and consumer prices came to be set uniformly and unilaterally by the seller, based on their calculus of what single set price would yield the most total profit from all customers. This was seen to provide fairness, in that everyone was treated equally, but customers lost their individuality and came to accept these set prices as a given—take it or go elsewhere.

- Some consumers still build relationships with sellers for reasons beyond price, but most consumers play the modern game of bargain hunting. Merchants generally decide between pricing for bargain-hunters or holding themselves out as premium providers, leaving it to the customer to self-select, depending on their price sensitivity. Behavior has shifted from communal norms to economic exchange norms that are focused on hard-headed *quid pro quo* and alienated from social values.

- *So, what started as a gain in transparency evolved into a cat and mouse game of mark-downs, discount codes, timed sales—a new opacity.* Even new methods that are made to sound win–win, like Priceline's "name your own price" (NYOP), were really structured as opaque zero-sum games more accurately described as "guess our price" (very different from the similar-sounding pay what you want [PWYW]).

Now we are in an age of one-to-one relationship marketing, deep tracking, and mass-customization. It is now well established that offers should be targeted and customized—but prices, still not so much. We recognize that prices might theoretically be individualized, but have no clear idea of how to do that. (Early attempts by Amazon were reportedly dropped after a backlash—perceived as unfairly imposed, and abusively manipulative—price discrimination as an evil.) Most businesses still customize price only to broad segments, such as by zip code, if at all (and those that are known to discriminate, such as airlines, are widely reviled for it).

The Paradox of Pricing "Experience Goods"

A postmodern pricing concept must deal with the paradox of experience goods. Regardless of cost or scarcity, the true value is not known until after the customer experiences the product/service, and that value varies widely from buyer to buyer. That value is unknown before the purchase. Modern pre-set prices often lead to buyer remorse (or windfall). If value is unknown until after the experience, traditional negotiation is not applicable at all (if negotiation is done after the experience, the buyer would have all the power to pay whatever they want, including nothing). How can we set a fair price after the value is known? *Only by negotiating a process, not a price. Only by agreeing on a process for pricing experiences will we achieve mass-personalization of prices and value-propositions.*

With the growth of digital offerings, we face a huge new kind of market inefficiency—to the point of an economic crisis in many content industries—and with significant loss of economic efficiency far more widely.

What we need is a new concept of what a price is and why. Key requirements of a price for the new economy are to accommodate and exploit:

- The asymmetry between mass-market institutional sellers and individual human consumers,
- The Alice in Wonderland economics of digital goods/services,
- The paradox of pricing experiences that cannot be accurately valued until after they are experienced,
- The power of mass-customization to find a new way to set prices that reflect the widely varying contexts of individual consumers,
- A relationship view, in order to maximize the lifetime value of a customer and encourage their loyalty,
- The new power of collaborative, computer-mediated dialog, to humanize institutions and re-engage communal norms of behavior, even between consumers and institutions.

FairPay shows how we can use automation (and computer-mediated communications) to solve these problems—to humanize rather than dehumanize institutional relationships with consumers.

FairPay Is a Rethinking of What a Price Should Be

The FairPay architecture seeks to find a new and better way to manage economic relationships. It throws off the tyranny of set prices, and balances the interests of both buyer and seller, while embracing the asymmetry—and efficiency—of institutional mass retail. FairPay lets us agree on a process for setting prices dynamically, after the experience is known.

For digital products—which can be costly to create, but nearly free to replicate—the old idea of a price as balancing supply and demand is no more meaningful than division by zero. Marginal cost is zero and supply is infinite. There is no inherent price derivable from classical supply-demand economics. The invisible hand can only flail about in the air.

We must go back and revisit the fundamental economics of sustainable digital business. If we frame the problem correctly, the path toward a solution emerges. How can a business make sufficient profit to be worth producing its product? How can it maximize this profit in this new kind of marketplace? How can it get customers to willingly pay a price commensurate with the value the seller provides, one that grants them a reasonable profit from each of a mass of widely varying customers? This seemingly paradoxical challenge requires a new paradigm—one that achieves a new balance of forces—a new invisible hand that can account for individual variation.

FairPay goes outside this box by shifting from a transaction view to a relationship view. Sellers need to find buyers who willingly pay fairly, in a way that generates a profit over the life of their relationship. Individual transactions can be unprofitable (even free), if that leads to a relationship that generates a fair profit from that customer over time.

The genius of freemium was to recognize "the power of free," but freemium just pushes the can down the road a bit. The product still has a set price, in this case two of them, applying "artificial scarcity" and the power of versioning: either free (a set price of zero) for the basic version, or some nonzero set price for the artificially scarce premium version. Neither is an efficient price. We need to look beyond our ingrained assumption that prices must be controlled and set by the seller before the sale!

FairPay creates a dynamic pricing process that lets buyers and sellers explore pricing levels jointly over time, building a relationship based on finding a level of payment that both parties consider fair overall. It does this by rearchitecting how prices are set. Instead of trying to find a price, we need to find a broader kind of agreement. *Instead of agreeing on price, we need to price out of agreement. Profitable transactions are just the trees—profitable relationships are the forest—and it is that forest that we need to see.*

Embrace the Variation—The Long Tail of Customers

Why is personalization of prices so important? Let's look at how value perceptions and willingness to pay vary from person to person. The Internet supports infinite variety. Just as Internet-based retailing allowed Chris Anderson's Long Tail of Items (catering to every interest) to be uncoiled, Internet-based pricing is poised to enable the uncoiling of a similar Long Tail of Customers (catering to every individual valuation and ability to pay).

Anderson's Long Tail is a tail of items ranked by units sold. As described in his *Wired* article and book (Anderson 2006a), online merchants such as Amazon and Rhapsody can stock many times more titles than brick-and-mortar stores, since they have essentially no limit to shelf-space. As a result, half of Amazon's total sales were accounted for by books that were not even stocked by a Barnes and Noble store. The well-known long tail curve (a Pareto distribution) shows a plot of the number of items sold, ranked by popularity (Figure 3.1).

Similarly, the Long Tail of Customers is a tail of potential customers ordered by price sensitivity—the price they are willing to pay for an item at a given time (a different Pareto distribution, known as a demand curve) (Figure 3.2).

Conventional set prices lop off this long tail by refusing to make sales to those unwilling to pay the set price. This eliminates a potentially significant market, out of fear that selling to those customers will cause the

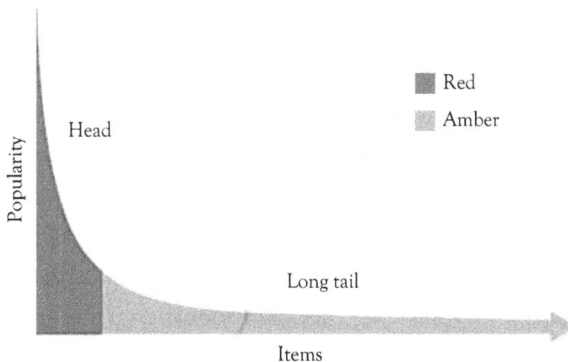

Figure 3.1 The long tail of items

Source: Adapted from Anderson (2006b), www.longtail.com/about.html

Figure 3.2 The long tail of customers

Source: Adapted from Anderson (2006b), www.longtail.com/about.html

other customers to demand lower prices. Conventional set prices also lop off the top of the tall head, since the seller gets only the set price, even from those who might be willing to pay more. So revenue is only the green box, even though there is a red surplus at the top of the head, and a long amber tail to the right. This shows the huge opportunity that FairPay opens up.

With FairPay, prices are individually set, based on what customers are willing to pay (subject to sellers using feedback on FairPay reputation to weed out free-riders who don't pay at an acceptable level). For digital products with near-zero marginal cost, the acceptable price level for large numbers of those potential customers might be relatively low. Most of these would be customers who do not buy at current prices, because they are not willing to pay that much—the Long Tail.

But because of their large number, this means that the Long Tail of Customers might turn out to contribute a very large portion of total revenue. Large numbers of customers at low prices, who would not otherwise be customers, can add up to a very large revenue increase.

Of course sellers might find that revenue from some of their current customers drops a bit (the curve may shift downward), because customers have freedom to pay less than the conventional set price. It may at first seem that sellers could not tolerate the risk that many FairPay customers might pay well under standard prices. That is the usual problem with PWYW pricing, but the FairPay control process is designed to maintain reasonable levels of pricing. And even though many current customers might pay a bit less, some can be motivated to pay more.

So the areas under the curve in red and amber potentially represent found money, money that would otherwise be left on the table. Why not sell to all who will pay more than the marginal cost of the product? Since prices are individually set, low prices to some need not imply low prices to all. If you can get customers to consider fairness, and to look at the rationale for this value exchange, most will accept that there are reasons why some deserve lower prices than others (more on that later). And even low-paying customers can add to advertising revenue, where that is a factor.

And why not try to motivate your happiest customers to pay a bit more? If you position that payment as going to a good cause (like museums and artists do), some who can afford to pay more will see reason to do so. Enlightened businesses recognize the value of likability and the inclination of people to be fair—this is a way to capitalize on being likable.

The Psychology of Price Variability

Let's look closer at the psychology of pricing on the long tail. Consumers hate to pay, or even think about paying, so content providers need to make it simple—but simple does not work well. Consider a content subscription Web site such as a newspaper or magazine, or a music or video service (but this applies broadly).

Conventional paywalls (even soft paywalls or other freemium models) face the dilemma that they put price as a hurdle in front of sales. Price too high and many potential customers will simply turn away; price too low and much potential revenue is left on the table. Pick your poison—there is no win–win, only bad or worse.

Add refinements such as versioning tiers of premium content or tiers by usage volume or other segmentation by market (artificial scarcity), and you add complication, and still have a step function that runs well below the price sensitivity curve. Even freemium still has this set-price hurdle when the customer wants to step up to the premium version. Remember that we are talking about experience goods, where the perceived value is not stable within a market segment, but highly dynamic, varying widely not just from person to person, but from time to time, depending on needs, moods, and reactions to dynamically varying products (such as news stories or video episodes).

FairPay may seem complicated, but that complication can be largely hidden from the customer. Yes, customers are forced to think about pricing more than once, but is that such a problem? Don't you think about pricing every time you eat in a restaurant and leave a tip?

With a simple paywall, customers must think about prices when they first hit the paywall. The hope is that they will pass through it, go onto an auto-renew subscription plan, and never think about it again (while the renewal money just rolls in). That will be the case for some, but others will balk (either up-front, or after they see they are not getting the value they want). Either way, the Procrustean paywall will cut off a huge portion of the potential revenue (whether the red head or the amber foot). One size just does not fit all. This simplicity is very costly to the seller— and a turn-off to many customers.

Is FairPay really more complicated or more of a hurdle? FairPay costs what the customer thinks fair. It is not rocket science, but gut intuition, guided by some conventions (much like tipping). The threshold for seller acceptance can be soft enough to remove all but a minimum of anxiety (as with tipping)—and once customers establish a reputation, price-setting actions can be infrequent and easy, and left on autopilot except as change is warranted. These psychological issues are important, and we will deal with them from many perspectives.

FairPay can hide a huge amount of complexity, because it is customer-driven and intuitive. Why not outsource to the expert? The customer can set a price that naturally reflects his needs, his usage, his valuation of the product and of the relationship, and his ability to pay—all with unlimited nuance and adaptation to current circumstance, and with hardly a thought. Fully evaluating the fairness of that on the seller side will take sophisticated decision rules, but the seller can begin with a simple, forgiving, fairness model to get close enough to true sensitivity, and later refine it to get even closer. This is just another aspect of customer relationship management (CRM), one that gets to the heart of the value exchange. Isn't it just this kind of customer relationship management that modern businesses should be seeking to cultivate?

The customer can enjoy a new kind of freedom, almost as much as free or PWYW. He no longer needs to wonder how much he will use and how much he will value it. That can be determined later, after he knows exactly what he got. If he underprices, the seller will be forgiving up to a point—and the worst that can happen is he is back at the paywall. There is no fear of buyer remorse to stop him from using a product he thinks he might value. … And the buyer and seller learn how to work together to find the fullest desirable and fair value exchange.

Price It Backward!—"Pay as You Exit"—The Wisdom of Alfalfa and Our Gang

FairPay turns many conventional ideas about pricing on their head, to the extent that, on first look, many people don't fully appreciate some of its key features.

Pay after the experience. One of the most powerful and underappreciated methods behind FairPay is stunningly simple. An amusing portrayal of this simple twist was in "Pay as you Exit," a 1935 episode of the very popular "Our Gang Comedies" series of short films (later shown on TV as "The Little Rascals" and now on YouTube). Alfalfa, one of the lead characters, was trying to drum up interest from neighboring school kids to buy tickets to a production of Romeo and Juliet to be put on by the gang. They were asking one-penny admission (this was 1935), and he was going on earnestly about how wonderful it was, but the potential attendees were having none of it. "How do we know it is worth a penny?" Alfalfa finally had a flash of inspiration and said, "I'll tell you what I'll do. If you like the show … *pay as you exit.*" A leader of the skeptical kids responded "OK, we'll take a chance," and so they all went in. The play was riddled with pratfalls that pleased the audience, and they all happily paid the one cent as they exited. Very simple, but very powerful.

FairPay extends offers forward in ongoing cycles of transactions, but for each transaction cycle, *the pricing decision looks backward.* FairPay price-setting is *retrospective.*

- Conventional prices are set *before* the buyer uses the product or service.

- With FairPay, the buyer sets the price *after* using the product or service.
- Setting the price before use exposes the buyer to risk of "buyer's remorse"—the buyer can only guess whether the value received will be as expected.
- So, setting prices forward (as is conventional) requires the buyer to take a leap of faith. As a result, the buyer must build a discount into what he is willing to pay, to compensate for the risk of a value surprise. Depending on the nature of the product, this risk (and the corresponding discount) can be significant. That is especially true for "experience goods" such as music, movies, and the like, and that risk can significantly reduce their potential market—buyers often will not take the risk at all. It also is significant when dealing with unfamiliar (untrusted) sellers for any kind of good.
- Even with many basic forms of PWYW, pricing is usually forward (even if set by the buyer). So up-front price-setting depresses PWYW results, since it leads buyers to set prices lower than they might do after the value was confirmed.

By setting prices backward, after the product or service has been used, the buyer has no risk of remorse. They know what they got and what value it delivered, so they can set their price based on that full value. Think about it: after you saw a great movie or played a great album several times, wouldn't you consider paying significantly more than the standard price for an average movie or album? Or with a poor movie or album, aren't you sorry you paid what you did, and wishing you could get a reduction or refund?

FairPay Cycles Go on Forever

It should be emphasized that FairPay is not just a temporary negotiation stage that leads to setting a fixed price after one or a few cycles. That could be done, but generally seems undesirable:

- Value considerations change over time.

- The beauty of FairPay is its ongoing adaptation, so why cut that short?
- The buyer's usage or needs may change, so their pricing should be allowed to change accordingly.
- The seller's product or service may vary in quality and value, so, again, pricing should vary accordingly.

Why not let the adaptive process inherent in FairPay keep doing its work to adjust for that? In its pure form it works in repeating cycles of an ongoing relationship, and that continues indefinitely—as long as both sides view it as fair. Of course this is not an absolute—FairPay is a just a framework, an architecture that can be adapted and used in hybrid forms as the situation warrants—but in general, it seems that there is little reason not to continue it.

The power of FairPay comes from being a repeated game. What matters is not any one cycle, but how the cycles motivate and converge on cumulative fairness over the relationship. If the game works, why end it?

Fuzziness in Pricing—Seeing the Forest, Not the Trees

A related feature of FairPay is its embrace of fuzziness. Just as we think of price as set by sellers, even if it need not be, we tend to think of price as exact, even though it need not be. By shifting our perspective to value over the course of a relationship, individual prices are reduced to individual data points that combine into a larger pattern. What matters is that a business relationship should be mutually advantageous and profitable over its life—that is, the forest. Individual transaction prices are just the trees that form the forest. We need to look beyond the trees, to see the forest.

Thus, it is not important that any one cycle generate a close approximation to an optimal price, as long as we get fair prices on average over any extended period. It is OK if the process is fuzzy and imprecise. The trick is just to keep nudging toward fairness (and to change the game for that customer if that fails repeatedly). Just as long-time friends accept that "it will average out" when settling up after a shared meal—splitting a check or alternating who picks up the tab—rather than adding up every item to get an exact allocation.

FairPay Negotiates a Relationship, Not a Price

FairPay is not a price negotiation, as such. It is easy to misunderstand the basic idea of these cycles. FairPay has similarities to a price negotiation process, in that it creates a two-way dialog about price, but (in pure forms) FairPay never leads to a set price that goes forward. For each cycle, the price set is always a retrospective price, set after using the product/service during that transaction cycle. Each new cycle is open to a new price evaluation by the buyer. *The negotiation in FairPay is on the underlying agreement on a process for seeking prices, not agreement on the individual transaction prices themselves. Focus on the forest, not the trees.*

There can be indirect negotiation. It is not yet apparent how widely useful it might be, but sometimes it might be desirable to add a layer with a new kind of indirect price negotiation. That negotiation is not about the price itself, but about the implications arising from a possible price—what potential buyer-set price level might lead to what further offers in the continuing relationship:

- *With FairPay, what the seller has to the power to negotiate over is not the price, but the offers that will follow.* There might be a negotiation dialog on the current backward price set by the buyer, and how that might relate to forward offers from the seller that might follow.
- The seller might react to a buyer's tentative (retrospective) price $X, and advise that if the buyer prices at that level, the seller will next extend basic offer A, but if the buyer sets a higher price $Y (for the transaction that is ending), the seller will extend a more attractive offer, B (perhaps including premium items, or some other perk), for the following cycle.
- Similarly, if the tentative retrospective price $X is considered unfair by the seller, the seller might advise that no further offers will be extended based on that price, but that if the buyer changes the price to $Y, then further offers will be made.
- The idea is to give the buyer more or less complete freedom to set each retrospective price as he sees fit, but to enable

the seller to provide guidance on how he will view that, *as it relates to further offers in this continuing relationship.*

- *The buyer retains full control of the price—what the seller controls is whether the relationship will be allowed to continue on that basis.*

Even in this scenario, future prices remain retrospective. The buyer is still free to pay whatever he wants after the next cycle. *What is negotiated is not the price for the next cycle, but only what price for the previous cycle will motivate the seller to make a particular offer for a next cycle.* (The customer can ignore that and do as he sees fit.) Similarly, even in the streamlined "autopilot" scenarios mentioned earlier, the customer retains the option to adjust autopilot prices in hindsight, if they decide that the fair value was not as expected.

A Price Discovery Engine

Some interesting insights into the power of FairPay were suggested by John Blossom, a strategy and marketing consultant to content providers, on his ContentBlogger blog (Blossom 2011).

It was John who reminded me of the Our Gang "Pay As You Exit" comedy episode that I had long forgotten. "It seems strange in a way to think that such an idea might actually help to save today's premium content sellers from their often rigid pricing regimes that seem to hold back their growth potential …." He goes on to explain how this derives from my Long Tail of Customers and highlights the value of FairPay as a "pricing discovery" regime. "The key to all of this is the profile data, of course, which is where Reisman may have his finger on a very valuable idea. FairPay is in essence real-time market research tool, enabling media providers to get more sophisticated insights into real willingness to pay for specific content under specific circumstances."

He adds that "It's not just a matter of knowing when to knock down prices for whom; it's also a matter of knowing when to mark them up, because one person's trash may have become another person's treasure. In such highly contextual markets, supply is perfectly matched with demand when the right content is available instantly at the right time."

His conclusion: "While it's very early days for the FairPay model, it could turn out to be a tool that content producers could use to experiment with pricing in new and exciting ways that could lead to higher margins and deeper market penetration for their content—two concepts that could lead to more happy endings on their bottom lines."

Win–Win Customer Journeys—With Dialogs About Value

It should be obvious by now that FairPay goes far beyond pricing to restructure the entire process of commercial relationships with consumers. This is consistent with other modern thinking about marketing, and one useful perspective on this is the idea of "customer journeys," a holistic view of ongoing customer relationships.

This emerging marketing paradigm provides just the context for a further step of proactively ensuring the journeys are maximally win–win. Some helpful background on this is in "Competing on Customer Journeys," by Edelman and Singer (2015). Their subtitle is "You have to create new value at every step"—FairPay suggests a way to enrich the customer journey to do that much more explicitly. They explain that:

> Rather than merely reacting to the journeys that consumers themselves devise, companies are shaping their paths, leading rather than following. Marketers are increasingly managing journeys as they would any product. Journeys are thus becoming central to the customer's experience of a brand—and as important as the products themselves in providing competitive advantage.

They suggest how this can enable "a 'loyalty loop,' … a monogamous and open-ended engagement with the firm." This is a big step forward in developing long-term profitable customer relationships, and it dovetails with the similar kind of continuing feedback loop that drives FairPay. The idea that FairPay adds is to insert "dialogs about value" into each cycle of the journey after the "enjoy" step—when the customer knows the value of the experience—and to adapt the pricing based on that. This enables participative personalization of the value proposition, as a simplified form of value-based pricing:

- Buy
- Enjoy
- *Value (the added step—dialogs about value, to personalize the value proposition)*
- Advocate
- Bond

Without this added step, the loyalty loop does not fully realize a central driver of engagement and loyalty—a proactively personalized value proposition that is win–win for both the customer and the firm. Without this we just perpetuate the idea that the firm decides on value propositions and tries to coax customers into accept them. Adding explicit value assessment into the loop engages the customer more deeply and enables the firm to serve the customer far more effectively. This element of customer participation builds customer loyalty by demonstrating the firm's commitment to learning exactly what each customer values in varying contexts, and seeking to deliver it by customizing the value proposition to match.

Edelman and Singer go to the threshold of this, just short of this one more step:

> We're now seeing a significant shift in strategy, from primarily reactive to aggressively proactive. … companies are designing and refining journeys to attract shoppers and keep them, creating customized experiences so finely tuned that once consumers get on the path, they are irresistibly and permanently engaged. Unlike the coercive strategies companies used a decade ago to lock in customers (think cellular service contracts), cutting-edge journeys succeed because they create new value for customers: Customers stay because they benefit from the journey itself.

The driving goal of FairPay is to make price reflect value, over time. When it comes to value propositions, firms remain coercive, effectively saying: "We give you this value package for this price. If you don't like that, how about this other value package for this other price? If none of our options suit you, we are just not listening—you will have to settle or go elsewhere." *FairPay dialogs about value open a new dimension of adaptivity and dialog to co-design value propositions based on individual context, needs, and value perceptions.* These dialogs about value become central to the journey, and a key driver of the loyalty cycle.

As the article explains, adding this focus on value does not just increase loyalty, but promises to dramatically increase profitability as well. The value step added by FairPay would bring value pricing directly into this journey—in a uniquely simple and lightweight form. This can enable a business to evaluate the value their services actually deliver to the customer, and to engage in dialog with the customer to share a portion of that value with the business. Rather than expecting the customer to take a risk that they will get a predicted value (which forces the consumer to discount the price they are willing to pay to allow for that risk), the business can design the journey to share the risk, measure the realized value, and share in that value. (More about this in the next section.)

FairPay is a very natural extension to the customer journey perspective. Edelman and Singer explain that "The move from selling products to managing a permanent customer journey has required mastering the four capabilities that all companies will need to compete: automation …; personalization …; contextual interaction …; and journey innovation …." The same four capabilities support FairPay as well.

As the new logic of customer journeys becomes accepted in marketing, the related new logic of FairPay and its adaptively win–win value propositions should become increasingly accepted as well. Different levels of FairPay empowerment may be applicable to different consumers and different business contexts, but a more explicit focus on value can benefit almost any customer journey.

Design Thinking About Customer Relationships and Business Models

The value-centered customer journey can be understood through the lens of "design thinking"—the recognition that our customer relationships should be subject to continuous redesign. Design thinking starts with user needs, and seeks to understand their journeys based on empathy maps. From that perspective, *FairPay dialogs about value become a GPS for empathy mapping*. FairPay helps move us toward better design thinking at two levels:

- As a form of design thinking, FairPay makes consideration of the user—and empathy and experimentation related to that—central to every customer relationship.
- FairPay can help drive entire businesses and industries to recenter on design thinking—by shifting the customer journey to drive dialog with customers to co-design value propositions—and to reflect that in pricing, so that it factors directly into the bottom line. That can drive everything else.

This is not unilateral design by the firm, but truly participative co-design. It is not occasional co-design, but continuous co-design.

This also relates to recent ideas made popular in the book, *Business Model Generation* (Osterwalder and Pigneur 2010), aptly self-described as "a handbook for visionaries, game changers, and challengers striving to defy outmoded business models and design tomorrow's enterprises" (and expanded on in a follow-on book, *Value Proposition Design* [Osterwalder et al. 2014]).

- The adaptive and dynamic nature of FairPay is itself a process for generating the details of business models (because it can take on the characteristics of many different models), and thus can help bake this idea of business model generation into core business processes.
- FairPay treats pricing as an ongoing process (to be designed), not a static endpoint (to be calculated). It offers an open-ended framework adaptable to almost any kind of pricing metrics and behavior desired. It is also a process for adaptive value proposition design.
- More broadly, it inherently links to all other business processes in a way that makes doing business a far more flexible and generative process.

The way to generate a business model in the Internet age is for the business to dynamically and adaptively generate its own right model—a model that optimizes value creation for both seller and buyer, for each relationship as it evolves.

Cloud of Value Marketing—New Big Data for a Customer-Centric Revolution

This idea of customer journeys and how to manage them leads us to another key development in marketing that FairPay exploits and expands on, the application of Big Data of all kinds, with growing focus on the Internet of Things (IoT). (Big Data refers to the growing availability of huge amounts of data that are now increasingly applied with advanced data analysis methods, starting with things such as Web clicks, searches, postings, texts, and tweets. The IoT refers to how even more Big Data is being derived from smart things—phones with sensors [including GPS], wearable health sensors, smart TVs, other appliances, cars, smart buildings, and beyond).

A perspective on how central this is to customer relationships comes from none other than Salesforce.com (Bosworth 2015). The idea is that IoT data can be marshalled and analyzed in the cloud to be acted on in real time, to enable a new level of business transformation, and more deeply intelligent, proactive, and personal customer engagements—CRM grows into a Marketing Cloud and the IoT Cloud feeds that. FairPay adds a new aspect to the IoT that we might think of as an IoT Cloud of Value.

We know how Web browsing and online content consumption creates a wealth of Big Data that is used extensively for marketing and to customize services, and customer relationships. What is less recognized is how this can provide rich data for personalized pricing, and how smart "things" create similar data even when seemingly offline. For example, the instrumentation of e-books provides great detail about how you consume them. That enables new kinds of pricing: How much you have to pay for a book can depend on how you read it—how much, how long, how deeply, how repetitively. That data is indicative of the value you receive from the book. Why should what you pay to read it not depend on how you read it? (See Chapter 10.)

From this perspective, FairPay can be viewed as having two fundamental and interrelated Big Data components:

- *Implicit signals of value.* These are drawn from conventional IoT data, including all of the usage tracking, activity, and clickstream data now widely used on the Web, and increasingly for any digital service.
- *Explicit expressions of value.* These are new kinds of data generated by the FairPay dialogs about value between the customer and producer. (These customer expressions can be partially validated by testing their consistency with the implicit signals of value.)

Applied together, these drive the FairPay process as it seeks to build mutually beneficial customer journeys, and generate dynamic pricing based on customer-context-specific win–win value propositions.

That enables a new kind of value-centered marketing that can transform how we do business—call it Cloud of Value Marketing. (And that, in turn, can lead to new kinds of Ecosystems of Value–more in Chapter 13.)

Computer-Mediated Commercial Dialog

The growing attention to these ideas of the customer journey, the Marketing Cloud, and the IoT Cloud reflects that customer journeys are increasingly computer-mediated. We have long seen it in pure e-commerce, and with the growth of "bricks and clicks" broadening into "omni-channel" retailing, it is penetrating what might have been purely physical retailing (as businesses reach out to our mobile devices using location-based services in and near their stores). Similarly the IoT Cloud enables computer-mediated contacts driven by any usage of any product or service.

Increasingly, we find ourselves in a cloud environment where computer-mediated commercial dialogs can occur anytime, anywhere, for any reason. If computer-mediated commercial dialogs are the norm, why not dialogs about value? Isn't that the heart of it all?

Testing FairPay at Low Risk

Of course any established business will want to do controlled testing in a restricted environment to learn how these methods work and tune the process, before putting mainstream revenues at risk. It will also be important to focus initial uses on the low-hanging fruit of selected customer segments who will most readily take to the cooperative behaviors of FairPay relationships. We will address a variety of strategies to start in phases and in controlled market contexts in Chapter 14.

Just to plant some seeds—some of the best opportunities for such limited trials are in:

- Retention "win-back" offers to customers asking to cancel their subscription. Customers who are known, and have proven interest in subscribing—who clearly value having a subscription but have doubts about the price/value proposition—can be offered a temporary trial of FairPay. Especially if the test is limited to users with low usage (for whom the regular subscription price may be inappropriately high), this makes good business sense all around.
- Acquisition offers to specially selected test populations.
- Premium level services, perks, and loyalty programs.

CHAPTER 4

Brief Example: Digital Content Subscription Businesses

We will examine a variety of practical business examples of FairPay in a range of industries in Part II, but let's take a quick look at a representative and important example. This is a subscription-oriented example. (FairPay also applies to item-oriented sales, when they are part of an ongoing relationship, as explained in Chapter 7.)

Digital content businesses of all kinds are increasingly shifting to ongoing subscription models for time-limited access to content. Subscription platform-vendor Zuora has nicely described this as "The Subscription Economy" and has described how this fundamentally changes business from sale of things, to ongoing access to services, with deep ramifications in customer relationships, finance, and core business infrastructure systems. Instead of buying content items and owning them in perpetuity, as distinct units, what is sold instead is a right to access a vast library of content, with run-of-the-house privileges ("all-you-can-eat"), but on a time-limited basis in which the right to access expires with termination of the subscription.

Examples of such subscriptions range across most of the big names in digital content, from aggregators such as Apple iTunes and Amazon Prime, to newspapers such as the *New York Times*, music services such as Spotify, and video/TV services such as Netflix, and HBO. Similar considerations also apply to non-content services such as Dropbox and LinkedIn. The aggregators are intermediary platforms for access to diverse content from many sources, while others are direct content or service provider businesses.

FairPay applies to both subscription businesses and more traditional item-oriented business that let customers download and own/use items in perpetuity (like iTunes and Amazon also do). Subscriptions most strongly depend on the continuing relationships that FairPay builds on and brings new dimension to. Such businesses already understand that customer lifetime value is critical to profitability, and focus intently on retaining and making the most of the customers they spend money to acquire.

- Subscriptions are a critical battleground for competing platforms and business models, one that could set the groundrules for monetizing digital content and services at the broadest level.
- Subscriptions get at the heart of ongoing customer relationships, and provide an aggregation structure that works for a broad swath of content and services.
- Subscriptions relate closely to the major pricing alternatives of free and freemium.

In the context of a subscription, the FairPay process unfolds on a (more or less) month-to-month or week-to-week basis (as illustrated in Figure 1.1):

1. As an alternative to the set-price freemium paywall, a selected customer can be offered a trial month of unlimited use of a basic class of service, on the basis that at the end of the month they will set a price for what they used, on a *Pay What You Think Fair* basis. The buyer will be told up-front that renewals for additional months (or weeks) will depend on whether the price they set is deemed fair by the seller.
2. As the process continues after initial use, buyers will be asked to set their price, and are given usage reports to remind them of what they used, and how that compares in quantity and value to typical subscribers.
   - The seller frames the offers and the pricing requests with background on standard set prices, suggested prices, and

typical FairPay prices actually set by other buyers, all with respect to the types and volumes of usage by the customer (such as basic and premium tiers).

- During each pricing cycle there are specific reminders that those who pay well will be offered added rewards (premium tiers, other perks) for future cycles, and those who pay less might be offered less.
- Buyers can be encouraged to give reasons why they chose to price as they did, including low or high usage, low or high quality, low or high value realized, economic circumstances (student, unemployed, retired, business use), and the like (primarily as multiple choice, for automated scoring).

3. As this continues, each buyer establishes a *FairPay fairness reputation* that characterizes how well and fairly they pay, and whether they do so consistently or erratically (with consideration of any relevant circumstances known or reported).

4. The offers to the customer after each pricing cycle are adjusted, based on their pricing fairness history.

- As long as the buyer sets prices that seem reasonable considering all these factors, the seller offers FairPay renewals, and the buyer enjoys the freedom of FairPay.
- The details of the offers and the process can be individually and dynamically tuned to encourage good payment levels.
- For those that fail to pay acceptably, it is back to the set-price paywall—after some level of warning or probation (at least for a time, possibly to be given another chance in the future).
- Thus the parties continually and jointly learn one other's views on the value of the service, and the expectations for fair pricing.

5. As buyers establish good FairPay reputations, the seller can extend more FairPay "credit" to include longer periods between pricing— providing more value that can be enjoyed before it must be priced. Price setting might gradually be reduced to a quarterly or yearly cycle

for established subscribers with good FairPay reputations, easing the burden of price setting, and extending more FairPay credit. (Payments might be monthly, even if price setting is yearly, for better cash flow and flexibility.)

In this way, FairPay takes conventional approaches to subscription pricing and stands them on their head.

1. The customer, not the seller, sets prices (for themself, as a market segment of one).
2. The seller selectively gates the offers to specific buyers, and thus manages the value at risk, at any given time, to each buyer.

This leads to more happy customers, plus more revenue to the provider to create quality services, based on the following:

1. Pay What You Think Fair and Price it Backward (after usage) largely eliminate risk of buyer remorse.
2. Customer price-setting accommodates a wide range of price sensitivities to ensure that anyone who gets reasonable value from a product/service can afford to buy it.
3. Sellers need not cut off potential buyers (who may not yet appreciate the potential value), only buyers who have proven (or are expected) to not value the service at an acceptable level.
4. The impossible task of setting a price that is "right" for all is replaced by the manageable task of understanding specific buyers and their sensitivities through a structured dialog. (Segmentation alone cannot be nearly as individualized, or as dynamic.)
5. FairPay provides a nuanced and individually set pricing "dial" that give readers real say in pricing, but leaves ultimate control of the relationship with the publisher.

Given its roots in the older pay what you want pricing method, it may take some thought to appreciate how FairPay is radically different, and can not only produce acceptable prices, but actual profit maximization—and do that with the necessary simplicity. We will address that in depth in the rest of the book, after the following simple example, and a review of some conceptual foundations.

A Sample FairPay Offer

The following is a sample of how a FairPay offer might be framed to a customer. For this simplified example we consider a newspaper that has decided to go to a freemium "soft" paywall model as is now common. Call it *The Times Journal*. An FAQ (frequently asked questions) is also suggested. (A skilled marketing communicator could do this better and more simply—this is just a suggestion of the kind of things that might be said.)

The Times Journal

Dear Patron of *The Times Journal,*

Introducing FairPay
Now you can pay what you think fair for *The Times Journal!*

As you know, *The Times Journal* online has been free, but we cannot continue to offer it without some subscriber payment and still provide the quality content you count on. Providing the journalism you expect from us is very costly, and more and more readers now get it online.

We are offering a conventional subscription plan, but are also experimenting with a new way to give our readers an unusual degree of freedom, largely on a "pay what you think fair" basis, as an alternative to more rigid conventional pricing methods.

We offer this as a special privilege to loyal patrons like you, and expect this FairPay plan to enable us to jointly build a relationship that is more "win–win." *The idea is that you and we agree to try to work together—so that we can learn to provide the value you seek—and do that at a price that you judge to provide fair value to you as our patron, and that we can accept as fair compensation to sustain our efforts to create the journalism that you value.*

Standard Subscription Plan:

As with many Web services, we now offer a simple pricing plan with two levels of service: a basic level of up to 10 articles per month free, with a subscription level that is required for more intensive reading (more than 10 articles per month). The standard subscription costs $4.95 per month. You may elect that subscription plan now, or at any time that you decide you want more than 10 articles in any month.

Special "FairPay" Plan:

As a preferred, more flexible alternative, we are selectively offering to you and other loyal readers what we call our FairPay plan. This monthly service works on the basis that you *"pay what you think fair"*—you are free to set the price each month to whatever level you believe to be fair, considering your level of use and the value of *The Times Journal* to you, at the end of each month.

The FairPay aspect of this plan comes in from the fact that we will review what you elect to pay each month (and your usage for that month, plus any feedback you provide in your pricing form), and will determine if you have been paying at a level that we can accept as fair. If so, we will continue to offer monthly renewals to you on this Fair-Pay basis. If not, we will warn you of our concerns, and if that does not change, you will be offered a regular subscription at $4.95 per month, or can simply revert to the 10 articles per month that are offered free with no subscription. (So in no case will you be worse off with FairPay.)

We view FairPay as a way for us to jointly learn how to exchange the value you get from us for the money you agree to pay us. Over time we hope to add more personalized offers, as we learn to understand you better. If you pay generously, you will get premium service levels and various special benefits personalized to your particular interests. If you pay less generously (considering what we know about your usage) you will get more basic service levels. Of course those who pay much less, at a level we cannot accept as fair, will be offered only the standard subscription plan.

Also, after a few months we plan to allow readers who pay at acceptable levels to set prices less often, going from monthly to quarterly, and later to yearly pricing reviews (unless you prefer more frequent reviews), so that the process becomes even easier. (You will still be able to adjust your current price at any time, if you feel that is warranted.)

We hope this FairPay plan will work well for you and for us. However, if after a period of experimentation we find that it does not result in sustainable pricing behavior from a sufficient number of readers, we may be forced to discontinue the plan. We hope you will find this plan attractive, and that we will be able to continue it and expand it. (We will maintain the set-price subscription plan, so you may opt for that at any time, should you so desire.)

Additional information is in the following *FairPay FAQ*.

Thank you.

Consumer FairPay FAQ (Sample, with Offer Letter)

[*Here we list only the questions—please see the full sample FAQ at FPZLink, with the answers, to further clarify how this process might be framed to consumers.*]

- Why are you offering this FairPay plan?
- What if I view only a few articles in one month?
- What if I am a heavy reader of many articles almost every day?
- What information will you use to decide what is fair?
- What if I am on a limited budget?
- What if few readers pay as much as you would like?
- Do your really expect people to pay more than the standard rate?
- Can my payments vary widely from month to month?
- Can I pay nothing at all?
- Might I get cut off from FairPay if I make a single misstep that you consider unfair?
- Isn't this monthly price-setting going to be a burden?

CHAPTER 5

Conceptual Perspectives

The Crisis in Pricing for Digital—Free? Paid? How Much?

The dynamics of networked commerce combined with the essentially free replication of digital offerings has created devilish problems that our current economics has yet to tame. Sellers have no clear rationale for setting prices and consumers feel they should not have to pay anything at all. Publishers seek to impose artificial scarcity (creating deadweight losses) and sometime impose practices that are downright customer-hostile. There is much debate and confusion over what should be free, ad-supported, and paid, and if paid, at what price?

The Value-Pricing Demon

The Prolog of this book proposed a thought experiment—hypothesizing an imaginary value-pricing demon that would know how to set optimally fair and efficient prices.

What good is a thought experiment? Einstein changed how we think about our world by doing thought experiments about what would happen when riding on a beam of light. Some influential thought experiments in physics involve imagining benevolent "demons" with special supernatural powers and knowledge: Laplace's demon, with its perfect knowledge of the state of the universe and all its natural laws, and Maxwell's Demon, with its ability to individually sort hot from cold molecules. Maybe we cannot build such demons in reality, but thinking about them can clarify our ideas and possibly point to approximations that can be built or applied—and can suggest directions for looking outside the box, as Einstein did to great effect.

Here we recap my pricing demon and expand on how its special knowledge can be approximated to power a system of commerce. Again,

my demon has perfect ability to read the minds of buyers and sellers to
determine individualized "value-in-use."

- The demon knows how each buyer uses the service, how
  much they like it, what value it provides them, and how that
  relates to their larger objectives and willingness/ability to pay.
  It understands the ever-changing attributes of current context,
  where the value of a given item can depend on when and how
  it is experienced.
- Furthermore, this demon can determine the economic value
  surplus of the offering—how much value it generates beyond
  the cost to produce and deliver it.
- The demon can go even farther, to act as an arbiter of how the
  economic surplus can be shared fairly between the producer
  and the customer. How much of the surplus should go to the
  customer, as a value gain over the price paid, and how much
  should go to the producer, as a profit over the cost of production and delivery, to sustain their ability to continue those
  activities.

This commerce demon could serve as the brains of a system that sets
prices that are adaptive and personalized—to set a price for each person,
at each time, that is fair to both the producer and the customer. We could
build services such as Amazon, iTunes, Netflix, or a newspaper subscription that were priced by the demon.

With such a demon setting prices, we could reap the cornucopia of
goods and services that the infinite replication of digital offerings promise
("information wants to be free") while still providing fair profits to the
producers ("information wants to be expensive"). Every customer who is
willing to pay more than the marginal cost of production would be able
to buy, while those who get and can pay for significant value would pay
appropriately higher prices.

This would be a win–win for producers and consumers, because it
allows producers to sell to all consumers who find value in the producer's
service, at prices that are dynamically personalized to approximate ideal
price discrimination. That leads to a near-maximum number of profitable and loyal relationships, to maximize total revenue and total value

creation. It also enables a near-maximum number of risk-free trials by consumers who think they might find value. All of this brings more value to more people.

As explained in the discussion of value-based pricing earlier, my demon has already been harnessed and proven highly successful—but this has been restricted to high-end, sophisticated B2B markets, and generally ignored in most other markets. So let's look more closely at how FairPay makes this concept workable in a simple, light-weight form suitable for consumer markets.

Driving FairPay Consumer Relationships

The FairPay architecture works as an emergent approximation of my demon. Not perfect, but still workable, as a process that uses simple procedures and dialogs to approach what the demon knows.

- FairPay shifts our perspective from individual transactions to a series of transactions over time in a relationship. That is what really matters.
- Instead of the invisible hand of supply and demand pushing the buyer and seller from outside, it brings an invisible handshake in which the buyer and seller agree to cooperate to seek a fair basis to exchange value. This can inform a new balance of powers, centered on "dialogs about value."
- *The buyer's power* is to set prices for a current transaction—"fair pay what you want"—with the understanding that he agrees to be fair, and that this is a temporary privilege that the seller will continue only as long as he agrees the prices set by that buyer are usually fair.
- *The seller's power* is to decide whether to continue these attractive offers, or not. That gives the buyer full buy-in on all prices, but motivates him to keep up his end of the bargain.
- Related data feeds in to the process, including the seller's suggested price to each buyer, the buyer's reasons for pricing higher or lower, and all of the increasingly rich individual details that digital system instrumentation can make available

about usage levels, patterns, and contexts, to inform *and validate* these dialogs.

- Based on all of that, the seller tracks each buyer's fairness rating, much like a credit rating.
- Consumers will warm to the idea of this pricing privilege, and will seek to protect it by maintaining their fairness ratings just as they do for credit ratings.

The result is an emergent process that seeks to discover the price, just as the demon understands it. The approximation may start out being quite crude, but digital sellers can afford a few unprofitable cycles in the early stages of each relationship, if that soon leads toward convergence on fair prices. As experience is gained, this will become a science of Big Data and predictive analytics—one that works to serve both the buyer and the seller.

So this FairPay process acts as an engine that approximates what the demon knows. It draws out the knowledge of the buyer, encourages truth-telling, nudges that with the views of the seller, and provides a context for the dialogs about value that lead to a fair split between the producer and customer surplus. Such a process can totally change the game of selling digital stuff, for more profit, and more value to society.

(Note that my demon takes us in a direction very different from the early vision of e-commerce "bots" that would negotiate prices on behalf of customers. The demon I propose is in some ways analogous to a bot, but instead of negotiating a single transaction, it works at a higher level that centers on value, not just negotiating power. Even if some forms of bot are important, such as the simple "chatbots" now gaining interest for business-consumer messaging, as from Facebook, this is still a far cry from a bot that negotiates prices on behalf of customers.)

Economics has generally ignored my demon, but it has been lurking in the background. First-degree price discrimination was defined by Pigot as applying some willingness to pay information in idealized monopoly situations—but has been viewed as not realistic for reasons such as arbitrage (those who bought cheaply could resell to others so they did not have to pay the full amount they would be willing to pay). I propose that the workings of FairPay enable something much like first-degree price discrimination, but instead of the entire surplus going to the monopoly, my demon shares it fairly between producer and customer. And since resale of digital services can often be made impractical, the arbitrage problem generally does not apply.

Adam Smith's Demon of Scarcity

As we saw, Adam Smith's invisible hand can be thought of as a similar demon that helps balance supply and demand in a market with respect to scarcity—and this has worked very nicely for many markets over many years. The beauty of the Smith's invisible hand is that it set prices in a way that worked not only at a micro level, but also as a basis for an allocation of resources for society at large. The whole edifice of market economics has been based upon this.

The core challenge of the economics of real goods and services is this allocation of limited resources: physical resources, labor, and capital. As Adam Smith said in 1776 in *The Wealth of Nations*, "… price … is regulated by the proportion between the quantity … brought to market, and the demand of those … willing to pay …." Smith went on to describe how

> … he intends only his own gain, and he is in this, as in many other cases, led by an invisible hand to promote an end which was no part of his intention. … By pursuing his own interest he frequently promotes that of the society more effectually than when he really intends to promote it. (Smith 1776)

So in the face of *scarcity across a market*, prices are set by the invisible hand to allocate the supply where it is most wanted. Hayek (1944, *The Road to Serfdom*) expanded on Smith to argue that an economy needs market prices as the only effective way to signal how resources should be allocated. Debate on how well this works for society continues, but it is widely recognized that it works to build wealth.

Is there something to replace that in the digital world? Here the challenge is not the scarcity of supply of existing items, but the ability to sustain the ongoing creation of new items.

- We now have freemium and other new models, but do they have any real economic rationale? Do they tell us how to allocate resources in a way that is good and efficient for individual producers and consumers, and across society?
- Many producers rely on some form of artificial scarcity as a way to sustain revenues, but put the accent on *artificial*—this has no fundamental basis, and creates no balance or fairness in resource allocation. That is a deadweight loss to society. It may help keep producers solvent, but is fundamentally inefficient.
- We also have the sharing economy, which recognizes digital abundance by emphasizing collaboration and open-source, but with concerns as to efficiency, effectiveness, and sustainability at scale.

An Invisible Handshake—Allocating Share of Wallet

It is time to replace the invisible hand of Adam Smith with something more suited to the strange and challenging nature of digital products. Think instead of an "invisible handshake," that draws producers and customers into a more cooperative, balanced, and productive relationship. It takes a handshake, because digital is a post-scarcity economics.

- What matters here is not a balance of demand and finite supply over a population of producers and customers in a single market.
- What matters is a compatible understanding of value between individual pairs of producers and customers who are free to act and build relationships without any production constraint.

Of course some scarcity is unavoidable. Our solution is not the extreme peer-to-peer "economics of abundance" that some now advocate—with its limited ability to motivate and sustain large-scale creation of value. The solution is to reimagine the socioeconomic contract between customers and the producers that create value for them, to ensure a business model for producers. To maximize the value produced, and the related entrepreneurial creativity, we need to motivate organizations that continue to be selfishly driven by a desire for profit. I suggest a new kind of market that rewards the creation of intangible stuff, based on this new socioeconomic contract—neither the limited motivational power of pure altruism, nor the deadweight loss of artificial scarcity. This new economy can evolve from where we are, starting now, with the FairPay architecture.

This new handshake is not on a transaction price, but on a continuing relationship. The contrast with the invisible hand is depicted in Figure 5.1. As shown, this fundamentally changes our economics from working across markets (horizontally, for the invisible hand on the left) without regard to past or future, to working through time (vertically in an ongoing chain, for the invisible handshake on the right), in relationships with individual customers.

Doing allocation in digital markets with this invisible handshake makes sense because *the game changes without scarcity of supply. What matters is no longer a dance of a market as a whole at a given point in time, but a dance of each customer with each producer over time.* So what should determine price?

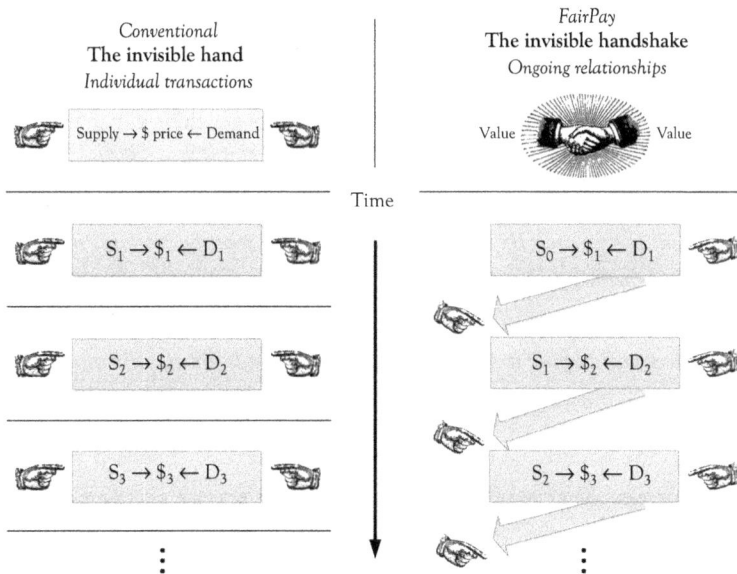

Figure 5.1 The invisible handshake

- Each producer can provide as much as is desired by each customer. There is no inherent supply constraint—all that matters is whether the compensation from that customer satisfies that producer (as providing a fair contribution to sustainable creation of more products).
- *Prices for different customers need not bear any direct relationship.* What does it matter if some pay more and some pay less? Maybe that depends on how much they want to use, what value they get, and how able they are to pay. (We are conditioned to think that price discrimination is unfair, but that is true only when unilaterally enforced through excess producer power, not if done for reasons acceptable to customers.)

The new allocation is not of supply, but of share of wallet. If each customer deals with a market full of suppliers for all their various digital products and services, the scarcity that matters is the scarcity in their wallet—how much can I spend on all my digital desires, and how do I split that among my providers?

- If I negotiate over time, in dialogs about value, to share the economic surplus of my digital purchases, I am forced to allocate my spending within some budget, across all my suppliers. I can do that any way I wish (to the extent that each supplier permits).
- If all customers do that, then all suppliers get their fair share of all the wallets for all their customers. *They sell as much as their aggregate market population desires, at a sum of individual prices, each the maximum that each market participant is comfortable allocating.*
- *Given a scarcity of nothing but wallet, what works for each individual pair in the market leads to a result for all pairs that approximates a market-wide optimum.*

Thus the handshake is essentially a moral contract between the individual parties. That may sound utopian, but it is a moral contract with teeth. There are strong practical incentives to adhere—and data that can be applied to help verify adherence.

- Digital products and services can be instrumented to generate detailed usage data that correlates to the actual value received.
- Both parties participate in ongoing dialogs about value, which add subjective insight, but still can be partially validated by the usage data.
- Based on these dialogs, the producer extends pricing "credit" to the customer. If the customer abuses this credit, they are given less credit, and lose some or all of the ongoing privileges of the handshake.
- This process generates customer reputation ratings for fairness with each producer. Since a good reputation rating has benefits (much like a credit rating), customers will seek to maintain it.

It is this balance of forces—the subject of the handshake—that governs the allocation of wallet (in an approximation of the wisdom of the pricing demon). Different producers can manage their own policies to make their handshakes very strict and demanding, or more loose and forgiving. Different segments of the population may play the game more or less fairly and honestly. But the process will adapt, and find workable relationships for most segments of the market. (And conventional pricing can be applied for those segments that fail the handshake.)

Some notes on scarcity:

- A secondary level of scarcity does remain—scarcity of resources needed for creating new services. My demon would factor that into its assessment of how to fairly divide the value surplus. It would maintain a touch of the old invisible hand, with that element of cross-market balancing of demand to gauge the proper supply of creative resources. Customers of services that are desired by few others would be expected to grant more share of the value surplus to sustain desired levels of ongoing creation—more than customers of services with large markets that share that cost more broadly. That would simply be factored into the dialogs about value, as just another aspect of value.

- Of course conventional set prices (or any pricing scheme at all) will also effect some kind of allocation of wallet. But is there any economically sound rationale?—it is arbitrary, crude, and not personalized (as the pricing demon would suggest), and thus results in significant deadweight losses (notably the value not provided to those who would benefit from and pay fairly for it).

- There is also the important case of ad-supported digital services that take no share of wallet. It seems increasingly clear that this is not sufficient to support most digital services but it will remain an important contributor. The handshake process can factor in the value of ad-viewing as one part of the compensation that offsets any monetary price, and thus takes less share of wallet. In fact, any aspect of value (attention paid to ads, personal information made available for sale, referrals, etc.) can be factored in as credits, as part of these dialogs about value.

A More Accommodating, More Sustainable Market

This invisible handshake provides the basis for a post-scarcity economy (at least for digital, and more broadly as discussed later). *The digital goods and services are not scarce, but the willingness of customers to sustain producers is scarce. The invisible handshake governs an allocation of that willingness to sustain.* To/from each customer according to his willingness and ability to pay. To/from each producer according to their ability to create realized and recognized value.

Like the invisible hand, the invisible handshakes between each of the individual pairs lead indirectly to a socially beneficial allocation. Like the invisible hand, it refers to an emergent process that by seeking local solutions, leads to globally optimal solutions.

- *The invisible hand* applies external market-wide forces (supply versus demand) to producers and customers at a given point in time (actually a short interval). It pushes them together to a market price. That pricing process indirectly leads toward a narrowly optimal distribution of scarce supply resources—but one that ignores broader "externalities."

- *The invisible handshake* is driven by an agreement between individual customers and producers to seek a mutually beneficial relationship. That binds them in an emergent process that generates prices over the course of the relationship, and indirectly allocates the wallet share of each participating customer to demand as much digital wealth as each is willing to pay for—at prices that work for each of them individually—to compensate producers for creating as much as each customer (and thus the total population) values—and reflecting any externalities that they both desire.

FairPay enables prices to reflect a much broader sense of economic value than is generally addressable in conventional markets. We expand on this in Chapter 22.

Participative Pricing, Co-Creation of Value, and FairPay as Co-Pricing

The points made here align with emerging trends in marketing theory that have caused FairPay to resonate with many researchers. Some of those trends are summarized in this section.

One of my first significant connections to researchers in marketing was Marco Bertini, a leading pricing scholar who had been researching "participative pricing" (Bertini and Koenigsberg 2014)—that led to our collaboration on the item published in the HBR Blog series in 2013 (Bertini and Reisman 2013), and a paper pending publication (Reisman and Bertini 2014).

More recently, I presented the concepts of FairPay—in collaboration with two prominent professors of marketing, Adrian Payne and Pennie Frow—to international leaders in an emerging branch of marketing theory at the Naples Forum on Service in 2015 (Frow, Reisman, and Payne 2015). This series is dedicated to the areas of Service Science, Service-Dominant Logic, and Network Theory, which all relate to recognition that business is really about the "co-creation of value" by customers, service providers, and other "actors," and that the production and sale of goods (which provide "value-in-use") is just one aspect of this larger concept of service. This has become a focus not only in academia, but in forward-thinking companies such as IBM.

The idea of a "Service-Dominant Logic" is in contrast to the "Goods-Dominant Logic" that developed over the past centuries—a "yesterday's logic" (Lusch and Vargo 2014). Now we are in a service-centered economy, and it has become apparent that the value of goods is really in how they enable a service—for example, the value of a car is not the physical product in itself—but in how it provides the service of transportation, in a particular use and context. Is it reliable, comfortable, safe, economical, fun? … in what mixture, to meet what needs? The value of services is understood to be "co-created" by the provider and the customer in a particular use-context. This has many important implications that have been the subject of an extensive body of work. Proponents of this thinking (including the related field of service science) have been among the most receptive to the ideas of FairPay.

(A note on terminology. Service-Dominant Logic suggests that there is no real distinction between *producers* and *consumers*, or *firms* and *customers*, and that all are just *actors*. I support that, and use those terms merely for their familiarity. Also, I mean *consumer* and *customer* to be interchangeable, but use *consumer* to emphasize reference to an individual person, rather than a business, as customer, without intending to mean one who consumes.)

My collaboration with Adrian Payne and Pennie Frow was tied to their work on business as co-creation (Payne and Frow 2013), and how that involves many co-creation activities, including co-pricing. The co-pricing aspect had not yet been well developed, partly because examples of co-pricing (like value- or outcomes-based pricing, and pay what you want (PWYW)) have been limited in applicability relative to other aspects of co-creation.

We think that FairPay has immediate potential to radically change business practices in a way that puts a powerful new form of co-pricing at the forefront of digital content businesses (as described in this book and in a paper we are writing).

Research Directions—Value-Dominant Logic and Cloud of Value Marketing

FairPay adds an important new research agenda in marketing and the behavioral economics of pricing, going well beyond the early work in PWYW and other participatory pricing practices. This book makes the case for experimentation—for proof of concept, and on to refinement (or to any pivots needed)—to move toward a new era in customer relationships with broad ramifications.

What FairPay adds might be thought of as a *Value-Dominant Logic (V-D L)—as opposed to yesterday's Price-Dominant Logic (P-D L)*. FairPay offers a process for seeking fair value, in which price becomes emergent from the buyers and seller's interactions over time. Thus price remains the metric of net value-in-exchange, on which our economy is centered, but now price tracks to value-in-context instead of being pre-set in ways that track poorly to value. This can not only transform business, but also make a better economics, because prices that track to value make the economy more efficient and productive. The central operational data for this Value-Dominant Logic is the Cloud of Value we spoke of earlier. So we can think of how this applies to business as *Cloud of Value Marketing*.

Another implication of this Value-Dominant Logic is that value should be very broadly defined to include all aspects that matter to the producer and the customer. Many of the current challenges in getting businesses to better address social values stem from the limited scope of prices, which currently do not reflect such broader values. We speak of corporate social responsibility (CSR) and creating shared value (CSV) and triple or quadruple bottom lines because our current bottom lines are missing many important components of value. Here again, FairPay provides a needed broadening—price is set in accord with value, including whatever social aspects of value matter to the customer. If the customer values broader social benefits, they can explicitly reflect that directly in the price they pay, which then adds directly into the bottom line. (Product/service prices could even have distinct components for customer value and broader value, all as set by the customer.)

Moving to a macroeconomic level, one of the open challenges of service research is that its focus on value-in-context works well at a microeconomic level, but does not translate well into macroeconomics—because value-in-context is hard to measure at a macro level. I suggest that the issue is that macroeconomics is centered on price, which in current practice correlates poorly with value. Revenue is the total of a firm's prices, but the *total of prices* now tracks poorly to the *total of value*; similarly for gross domestic product (GDP). If we can get prices to track better to value, then our whole economics will be driven by that, and will work better.

CHAPTER 6

A Top Management Perspective

The commentary on FairPay that I published in the HBR Blog series with Marco Bertini in 2013 (Bertini and Reisman 2013) provides a perspective on how FairPay builds on and extends key directions in modern consumer marketing.

It begins with a brief review of the challenges of selling digital content and the turmoil in the content industries, as they face the conflict between free and paid, to suggest how companies can cope with these new challenges and opportunities by moving toward a new architecture that moves the exchange between seller and buyer from the transactional to the relational.

Starting at a broad, strategic level, the article explains how this architecture reflects three key ingredients of today's social marketplaces:

1. **Empowerment**. Companies are embracing the idea of delegating activities to their customers. We see this in marketing with product development and advertising, mostly. But what about monetization? How about letting customers participate—at least to some controlled extent—in price setting to raise their level of engagement?

2. **Dialog**. Gaining customer feedback is intuitive. But how often does the seller get involved and create a true dialog? And, even if there is discussion, how often is it tied directly to the pricing process? Modern e-commerce systems can enable rich automated value-focused interactions, but this capability is underused.

3. **Reputation**. Integrate the idea of social capital in the monetization approach. You can do this by creating a reputation score that relates directly to customers' conscious use of the pricing power granted in point 1. Importantly, this score evolves over the course of multiple transactions.

Those are general, flexible strategies that can be configured in many ways. The article then suggests FairPay as a more specific configuration of these strategies:

1. **Empowerment.** We take an extreme view: buyers first experience the product and then have the power to pay whatever they wish, including zero. The timing matters because (a) customers should know the product they are asked to sacrifice money for, and (b) it fosters reciprocity, a strong social norm. Moreover, there is a constraint in place to avoid free riding: companies retain the right to make future FairPay offers (i.e., they can take away a customer's price-setting privilege).

2. **Dialog.** Firms suggest reference prices to anchor a customer's price offer and can provide reports to remind people of the value received. Customers are asked to justify the prices paid by indicating their reasons. Firms respond with counterarguments. Importantly, this dialog is structured for scalability and personalization through the use of modern choice architectures. The technology is there.

3. **Reputation.** Customers have a fairness rating. Choice architectures are then applied to segment customers in terms of fairness (and other attributes) and apply "carrots" (relating to product tiers, perks, etc.) to improve profitability or "sticks" (the threat to remove a customer's price-setting privilege) to at least sustain it.

To put this in the more concrete terms of its operational core, FairPay applies a fundamental mechanism of balancing (= *Dialog*) to two elements: on one side, customer post-pricing power (price it backward, after the experience = *Empowerment*) and on the other side, business power to control what further offers are made (extend it forward, if the customer is being fair = *Reputation*). That turns commerce into a repeated game, in which it is in the customer's interest to price fairly, building social capital, so the seller will continue to make further offers that continue to grant them pricing empowerment. This book explains why and how to do that. It also explains the extensive body of experience that shows that consumers will naturally take to it, once they see the empowerment it offers—and shows how companies can readily learn how to apply it (with ever-growing sophistication).

The promise is dramatic expansion of markets and profitability, and increases in customer loyalty and lifetime value.

Overall, the FairPay architecture can be viewed at a hierarchy of levels:

- *Level 1: Adaptively seeking win–win*: The general strategy of setting dynamically personalized pricing—based on adaptively seeking win–win pricing and value propositions, for specific customers in specific time-varying contexts, as understood through a Cloud of Value. It seems that sooner or later this has to become the best basis for a productive economy.
- *Level 2: The core FairPay cycle (the invisible handshake)*: The fundamental process for balancing.
    - o the power of customers to do post-pricing (price it backward) with
    - o the power of a business to control whether and what further offers are made to each customer (extend it forward?).

    This seems the only promising process architecture for achieving Level 1—one that promises to work very well once it is tested and refined.
- *Level 3: The particulars*: How and where FairPay complements or supplants other pricing techniques, and what specific forms it takes in varying business and market contexts—and how that evolves from low-hanging fruit to broad use. Here we can only guess, but time will tell—if we do reasonable experimentation to get from here to there.

Entrepreneurial Opportunity—Platforms, Databases, and Network Effects

FairPay can be implemented entirely within individual businesses, but it can also be provided as a database and platform service to multiple businesses. The FairPay dialogs about value create a new kind of Big Data—a Cloud of Value—with new detail about individual customers' value perceptions and fairness that can be very valuable within and across businesses—serving much like a credit rating. The software needed to implement FairPay can be provided as a platform services to many merchants or service businesses. Just as there are now Subscriptions as a

Service platform offerings, this could extend to *Pricing as a Service*. Both the platform and the databases offer significant network effects and first mover advantages. This could be a huge entrepreneurial opportunity, and lead to new kinds of *Ecosystems of Value*. (See Chapter 13.)

Making It Happen—Adaptively Seeking Win–Win

Every company should be thinking about this new logic for seeking prices that map to value—as win–win for both customers and producers. Fair-Pay provides an architecture for an ongoing process that seeks to do that, to enable a new kind of *Cloud of Value Marketing*. The particular processes I propose are just a starting point framework—they need to be tested in specific contexts, to enable learning that will lead us to variant processes that will work increasingly well. *One way or another our path forward is to apply some form of Cloud of Value Marketing that is adaptively win–win. That path should lead to more value for all of us. The critical questions for top executives are where, when, and how.*

PART II

Applications in Industry

In this section we dig in to how FairPay works in practical business use cases. First chapter adds key details on the core processes of FairPay and how they work across industries—then the next series of chapters examines specific industries. Jump ahead if you want, but come back here to fully understand the processes that make FairPay work. FairPay is such a deep paradigm shift from what we have come to accept as how business works that it takes a bit of reorientation to fully appreciate how and why it works. (In Section III, we briefly survey how FairPay compares to conventional pricing methods.)

CHAPTER 7

Making It Work— Operational Details, Tools, Continuous Learning and Adaptation

Why Would Anyone Pay If They Don't Have to?

The answer is simple: Buyers who do not pay will not get further offers.

This is the first question many people ask on hearing of FairPay—given its superficial similarity to Pay What You Want (PWYW) pricing. But FairPay is very different. It is a repeated game, with a balance of powers—if you want to keep playing you must pay enough to keep the seller satisfied enough to let you do that. With FairPay, there are consequences for not paying—much as there are for having a poor credit rating.

Guiding FairPay Pricing for Control and Predictability

The objective is not just getting them to pay—but getting them to pay enough—in a way that is manageable and predictable enough for a sustainable, ongoing business.

We will look in later chapters at the background on PWYW, and the clear evidence that it is really far more effective and widely applicable than one might think. For now, let's just take it that most people do pay even when they do not have to, and that PWYW can be very profitable in selected promotional or other special uses, but is often not profitable enough for regular, sustainable use in an ongoing business.

FairPay is very different from conventional PWYW, because it turns it into a repeated game, adding a feedback and control process that give the seller powers over the repeating cycles that fully balance the single-transaction pricing power of the customer.

- *FairPay turns pricing from a one-time game, in which there is no real penalty for underpricing, to a repeated game.* Because of that, customers benefit from continued play, and so are motivated to maintain a good fairness reputation, building social capital at some cost, to retain the option to continue. PWYW—and most other pricing methods—fail to apply this powerful lever to ensuring fair cooperation.
- *Further, in its detailed operation, this control process can be architected to apply many tools of behavioral economics to nudge customers to pay fairly.* As we will explain later, few uses of PWYW have been very sophisticated about framing offers and expectations. Modern marketing methods have huge potential to make such processes work with far greater control and predictability.

FairPay Process Dynamics—The Core Feedback/ Control Cycle

The heart of the FairPay process is the core feedback/control loop that we first saw in Chapter 1. (We repeat Figure 1.1 here, as Figure 7.1, for ease of reference; Figure 7.2 expands on that in a section that follows.)

This feedback/control loop reframes the "pay what you want" element of FairPay, shifting it to "pay what you think fair" (or "fair pay what you want," which is what inspired the name FairPay)—and enforcing that fairness. As we will see, there are many variations on this basic loop that can be applied, but there is a simple elegance to the balance of forces this loop provides (Figure 7.1).

The key steps of the cycle are:

- *Gated FairPay Offer*, from seller to buyer: FairPay offers are *gated* by the seller—selectively offered as a privilege, and restricted in value and duration—to limit seller risk.

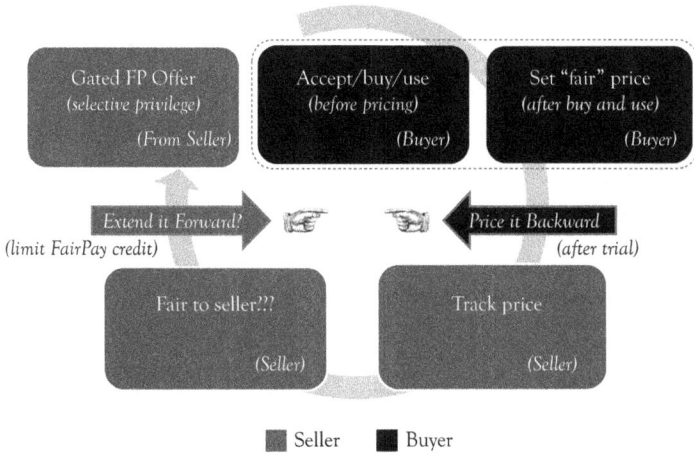

Figure 7.1 FairPay participative process

- *Accept/Buy/Use*, by the buyer: The buyer accepts an offer, buys, and uses a product/service long enough to have a reasonable sense of its value.
- *Set "fair price,"* by the buyer: The buyer is entirely free to set the price ("Fair Pay What You Want"), in his sole discretion, which the seller must accept. (Of course variant forms of Fair-Pay can pre-specify seller-imposed constraints on the price, such as a minimum "floor" price, if that is made clear at the time of the offer.)
- *Track price*: The seller tracks the price set by the buyer, along with relevant context details.
- *Fair to seller?*: The seller decides if they view the price as acceptably "fair," considering the context.
  - *If so*, the seller makes further FairPay offers, continuing the cycle, and extending its benefits commensurately.
  - *If not*, the FairPay process ends (possibly after a warning or probation process and a limited number of further cycles), and the buyer is only offered conventional fixed-price sales.

Here we see the essential difference between FairPay and conventional PWYW offers. Unlike the asymmetric buyer-side power of conventional PWYW offers, with the level of unfairness that often results, the seller has an equal and complementary power to balance that. The buyer knows up-front that FairPay offers are a revocable privilege, and if he does not set the price reasonably, that privilege will end. That is the essence of the repeated game that drives cooperation and equity. Conventional PWYW lacks this feedback/control process—the gating, tracking, and fairness evaluation. PWYW offers are made to anyone, without restriction, so that even those who have a history of free-riding can continue to do so with impunity.

The core balance of these forces is seen in the dialectic of the two arrows:

- *Price it Backward* reflects the *buyer's power* and privilege of setting the price after he knows what the product was actually worth to him (unlike the conventional case where the price is set in advance and so there is risk of buyer's remorse).
- *Extend it Forward* reflects the *seller's power* to gate the FairPay offers, and to limit them as a privilege granted only to those who set prices fairly.

This process is *participative* in that the buyer has real say in the pricing, but the seller still gets to limit his risk. This participative process ensures that both parties continue only if they agree that the prices are fair (at least over a series of cycles). This creates a process of constant learning and adaptation, and the longer this continues, the better the parties understand one another, and the closer the offers and prices get to an ideal win–win value exchange.

Thus FairPay realizes the economic ideal of individually *differentiated* prices that correspond to the utility and price sensitivity of each buyer in a way that avoids the feeling of unfair "*discrimination*." Price discrimination is merely a problem of roles and perception—there is nothing inherently wrong with price discrimination, if it is done transparently and fairly—it is beneficial to the general welfare. Since with FairPay, it is always the buyer who sets the price, the discrimination is inherently acceptable.

This participative nature is what gives FairPay real power to enable a business to build a deep win–win relationship with its customers, to achieve high loyalty and sustainable competitive advantage.

Framing—Expectations of What a Fair Price Should Be

Framing is one of the key methods for making FairPay effective. It is the process of shaping ("framing") expectations. Framing is the toolbox used to manage how FairPay offers are presented, and what expectations on pricing are set—both up-front and throughout the dialogs on value—to serve as a key technique for managing customer response.

One of the best ways to manage FairPay pricing may be to *draw on a suggested pricing structure to frame the setting of FairPay prices to be done by the buyer*. Here is an example of how that can work for the seller.

1. When making the offer, provide a preliminary suggested price schedule, so the buyer has a clear idea of what you will be expecting. The buyer can still be completely free to price as he feels fair, but will know the seller's reference point.

2. After usage, provide the buyer with *a specific suggested price based on that schedule, and adapted to reflect details of the actual usage*. The schedule might be a single price, or might provide whatever level of structure you think the buyer might grasp. The suggested structure might explicitly take into account such factors as usage/volume levels (counts/times, etc.), categories of product/service used (basic or premium, etc.), buyer demographics (business/consumer/student/ retired, etc.), indicators of value obtained, adjustments for any problems, and so on. (This schedule could be customized to the buyer in response to what is learned about him, but showing some information on how it varies, and on how others set their prices can help frame the buyer's understanding.)

3. Provide a price-setting form that presents the suggested price and its rationale, and asks the buyer to set a price as the suggested price plus or minus a differential—whether a percentage or a dollar differential. This use of a differential is not essential, but it makes it clearer how the price varies from what was suggested, and facilitates computations of fairness for items regardless of absolute value—for example, a price for a song suggested at $0.99 or an album suggested at $9.99 can each be set buy the buyer as –10 percent (or +10 percent), with essentially the same level of fairness.

4. Include in the form a set of multiple choice (and optional free text) inputs to enable the buyer to explain the reasons why he thinks his differential is fair. Depending on what is already in the suggested price rationale, these reasons might relate to additional aspects, such as usage/volume, product value perception, buyer circumstances, problems, and so on.

5. Determine a fairness rating for the price (the differential), as explained by the buyer—unfair, marginally fair, fair, very fair, generous, and so on.

6. Provide feedback from the seller back to the buyer on the seller's view, in terms of this fairness rating. (This can be clear and explicit, but can also be left fuzzy, or just implicit in how the offers are made.)

This provides a shared frame of reference that can guide the buyer to price more or less closely to the suggested amount, and provides a basis for communication and judgment as to the fairness of any differential.

This structuring works within the broader FairPay pricing feedback process, in which sellers communicate back to the buyer regarding fairness, and determine whether to make more and better product/service offers, or to warn and restrict the buyer, or to disqualify them from further FairPay offers. That broader process provides the primary method of control:

- The seller controls the offer management process to stage their offers to form a series in an ongoing relationship (such as a subscription).

- That staging enables the seller to limit the value at risk (at any given stage) to buyers who have not established a reputation for paying fairly, and to extend that as the relationship warrants. Offers can be managed to limit the value of any unfair exceptions, and to minimize their number.

- Seller policies can be varied to be strict or lenient, to whatever degree appropriate to a given situation.

With this combination of offer framing, suggested prices, and feedback-driven incentives to price fairly, sellers should generally obtain FairPay prices that average very near to their suggested prices (if the suggested prices are fairly reflective of the actual context of use, as it varies from buyer to buyer, and from time to time).

Of course the idea here is to guide the buyer, but not to be deaf to buyer feedback. FairPay is a dialog about value, and it takes two to have a real dialog. If there is a pattern of buyers pricing below suggested values in any context, that is an indication that buyers are not satisfied with the value received in that context. Such a situation should be understood as a disagreement as to value that the seller needs to address, whether by changing the perceptions of the value, the realities of the value, or the price suggested in exchange for that value.

Keep in mind that this may work best where a conventional set-price offering remains the default for those who do not price "fairly." I suggest generally pegging the suggested FairPay prices somewhat below the set (non-FairPay) prices to give the effect of a *relationship discount* to those using FairPay, and thus add to their incentive to maintain that FairPay privilege. That provides a "stick" to enforce fairness, but as we see in the next section, we can also add "carrots" to put a more positive spin on things.

A Richer View of the FairPay Process

Building on that core cycle, we can add important features to make this process more compelling. Perhaps most powerful is to build in a richer incentive structure (with both carrots and sticks), using product/service tiers (Figure 7.2).

1. First, we start at the bottom with the conventional "Set-Price Zone" in which prices are pre-set by a potential seller as usual. While this might be eliminated in a pure FairPay world, it seems that it might always be desirable to retain this as a fallback for those who do not price fairly, and to maintain a reference price to backstop the FairPay process.

2. *The basic FairPay cycle begins at the lower left*, entering what we call the FairPay Zone. FairPay offers can be introduced more or less selectively, to specific buyers, as a special pricing privilege. There, a potential buyer is first presented with a FairPay offer from a potential

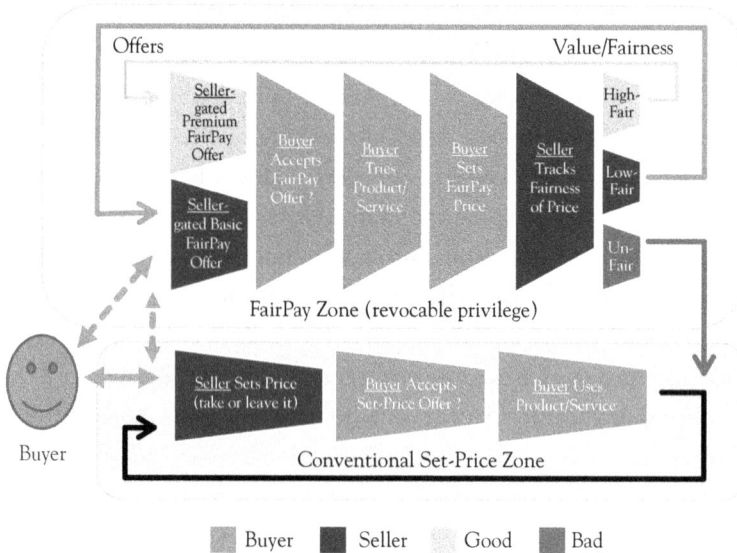

Figure 7.2 FairPay process with incentive tiers

seller, subject to basic qualification criteria. This could be a known buyer who is viewed as likely to be receptive and fair, or an unknown buyer (prospect) who will be tested in early cycles of the process. The initial offer may be limited to basic services, as the buyer and seller get to know one another with respect to FairPay pricing. The basic principles of the FairPay Zone would be introduced, including how enhanced offers tiers reward fairness and generosity, as we see at step 7.

3. The buyer can accept the FairPay offer, with the understanding that it is on the basis of *Pay What You Think Fair* (= *Fair Pay* What You Want), with the price to be determined after initial use.

4. The buyer tries the product/service, and *learns its actual value to him at that time.*

5. The buyer is then reminded to set his FairPay price for that transaction—to "Price it Backward"—and invited to give any explanation that might be relevant (preferably in multiple choice form). The seller might include a report on usage and suggest an individualized value-based price, to help frame an anchor price. Again the reward of enhanced service tiers is emphasized.

6. The seller tracks that price and any explanation, and relates it to any prior history for that buyer to determine a *FairPay Reputation* for the seller.

7. *Now we get to the added layer of enhanced product service tiers.* Based on that price and the FairPay Reputation, the seller decides whether to make further offers (now or in the future). This can be done at various levels of granularity—for example, in a simple two tier case:

   o If the price is considered *Low-Fair*, *basic offers* are continued.

   o If the price is considered *High-Fair*, offers are continued, and even better *premium offers* might be extended (including higher value products/services, special perks, more time to try before pricing, etc.). *Use of a premium tier gives added incentive for the buyer to pay the maximum he thinks fair.*

   o If the price is considered *Un-Fair*, the FairPay privileges are (eventually) revoked, and the buyer goes back to the conventional Set-Price Zone (at least for a time). *That gives the buyer an incentive to be at least minimally fair.* (Such downgrades can be handled gently, such as with a probationary period in which the customer is first warned that more favorable pricing is needed to maintain the FairPay privilege beyond one or a few more probationary cycles.)

Again, this process is generally best applied in combination with conventional set-pricing (as with a paywall). That gives a clear alternative, and clear consequences for not paying at a level the seller can accept to be fair. It establishes a clear *reference price* to use as an anchor for Fair-Pay pricing considerations (it probably should not be framed as being a minimum price, since there may often be good reasons to pay less, and doing that might make it harder to motivate people to pay more than that without giving them extras). The conventional pricing remains a real alternative for any buyers for whom the FairPay process is ill-suited or unappealing.

This simple approach can take on many forms, and provide great amounts of flexibility and adaptability. (And of course good marketing communications skills should be applied to framing the operation of this choice architecture in the most customer-friendly light.)

A simpler view of the complementary nature of these strategies is in the following diagrams. First we start with a conventional freemium service, a simple "soft" paywall, with limited free product, and a set-price paywall for usage beyond that (such as for a newspaper subscription). As shown in Figure 7.3, there might be multiple tiers of services, with a higher fixed price for the premium tier (to the right).

Then we add the FairPay Zone above that (Figure 7.4).

These diagrams hide the details of the FairPay processes, and simply show it as a fuzzy FairPay Zone, with prices running along a spectrum. The idea is that we move beyond a paywall with set prices, to apply a

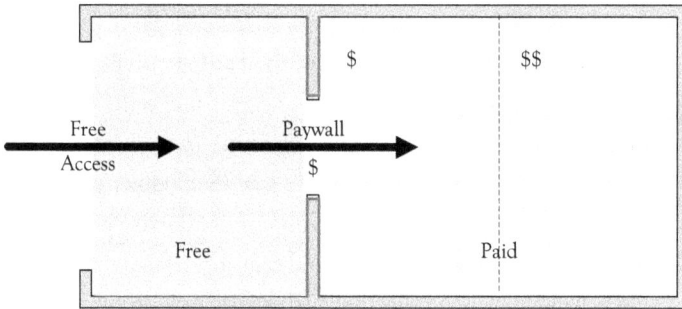

Figure 7.3 Conventional paywall

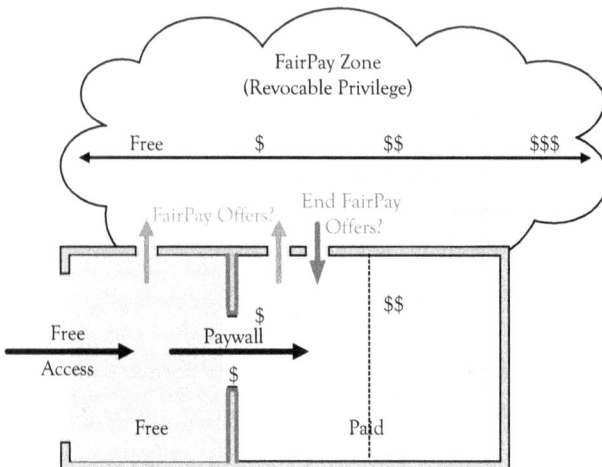

Figure 7.4 Paywall plus FairPay Zone

flexible spectrum of prices (vs. products/services) that adapts to whatever the buyer and seller agree to be fair.

If this is done with well-considered policies, it will be sustainably win–win. Once a buyer is invited into the FairPay Zone, he will want to retain the privileges that go with that, and will seek to keep the seller satisfied, so that privilege is not revoked. (And when this is not the case for a given buyer, the extent of abuse can be limited.) This balance of forces increasingly converges over time to enable the seller to obtain the maximum price that each participating buyer thinks fair, and thus to maximize revenue over the entire addressable market. That is how FairPay works as a repeated game that is continuously adapted to seek to continue on a win–win basis.

How to Set Policies?—Continuous, Pervasive, Multivariate Marketing Experiments

People often ask about how these policies and parameters should be set, and I answer based on my expectations of what will work in likely contexts, drawn from several years of developing these ideas. This book makes suggestions, but these are only initial presumptions—bound to be revised and enhanced as experience is gained with real customers in real business contexts. Strategies will vary with the industry and business, and from customer segment to segment. They will also vary over time, as both businesses and consumers become familiar with this new logic and how each other behave as they come to better understand it.

Sophisticated marketers will see how this process is well suited to emerging strategies for targeting and testing of offers with multiple variables, and the application of Big Data analysis and predictive analytics. Instead of doing A/B or multivariate testing or similar marketing research as a side activity of limited scope and duration, FairPay builds it into routine processing—into every offer and every price for every transaction (subject to some basic simplifications).

The range of parameters to be considered is summarized in the following points. Some apply to both FairPay and traditional PWYW (and other strategies), and others are more specific to the added processes of FairPay. FairPay is not one specific method, but a general architectural framework. Specific implementations of FairPay can take widely vary-ing forms. We will be looking at some of the most interesting of those variations.

Reviewing the overall perspective outlined earlier, there is a hierarchy of levels to this architecture:

- *Level 1: Adaptively seeking win–win*: The general strategy of setting dynamically personalized pricing—based on adaptively seeking win–win pricing and value propositions, for specific customers in specific time-varying contexts, as understood through a Cloud of Value. It seems that sooner or later this has to become the best basis for a productive economy.
- *Level 2: The core FairPay cycle* (*the invisible handshake*): The fundamental process for balancing
  - the power of customers to do post-pricing (*price it back-ward*) with
  - the power of a business to control whether and what fur-ther offers are made to each customer (*extend it forward?*).
  This seems the only promising process architecture for achiev-ing Level 1—one that promises to work very well once it is tested and refined—but perhaps other methods will become apparent as we learn more.
- *Level 3: The particulars*: How and where FairPay complements or supplants other pricing techniques, and what specific forms it takes in varying business and market contexts—and how that evolves. Here we can only guess, and time will tell—if we do reasonable experimentation to get from here to there.

Level 1 is clearly the direction for the future. Level 2 promises to be the way to get there—and even if getting Level 2 to work well involves some bends in the road, trying it and learning from it will help us find the path to Level 1.

At the same time, remember that limited negative results at Level 3 should not be taken as conclusive, just as limited success with PWYW does not mean that there is not something to work from there. Given how radically new and unfamiliar these methods are to both businesses and customers, we need a reasonable period for learning—and to raise broader understanding about how these methods can and should work. I expect that important levels of initial success can be achieved with just months of serious and skillful effort—but even if it takes years, it will be worth the journey.

A Flexible, Extensible Architecture

An important aspect of FairPay as an architecture is how flexible and extensible it is. As we will see in Chapter 15, this architecture has many levels and many policy parameters that can be varied. These can be tuned to create a wide spectrum of behaviors, using a variety of choice architectures, relating to such aspects as:

- Gating, nudging, warning, dispute-resolution
- Up-selling, down-grading
- Liberal or tight control

It can coexist with conventional pricing, such as varying what method is used with what segment based on their fairness behaviors. It can also be tuned to behave in ways analogous to conventional methods—but with better personalization—to parallel conventional behaviors relating to:

- Freemium and paywalls (metered/soft)
- Tiers, segments, and dynamic/usage pricing
- Personalized mixes of customer revenue and advertising.

We will also examine a range of strategies for how FairPay can be phased in:

- Applying it first to limited, controlled populations in confined aspects of a business, to minimize risk during the initial learning process.
- Gradually adding levels of sophistication and control, so customers can become acclimated, and businesses can learn how controls should be developed.

What Kinds of Business Should Consider FairPay?

The following chapters look at representative examples, but at the broadest level, FairPay is applicable to any business that seeks ongoing relationships with customers. It is less well suited to short-lived commercial relationships, since there is no incentive to play the repeated game, and little opportunity to learn how to find a win–win level of fairness with a specific customer.

There are two major modes for selling goods or services that FairPay applies to in slightly different ways (many businesses may include both):

1. *Subscription relationships.*

   These offer recurring access to ongoing services, and so are an obvious and natural place to apply FairPay. Examples include all kinds of content subscriptions, whether single source, like the *New York Times* or *CBS*, or multisource like Netflix or Spotify, and similarly for other kinds of services such as Facebook, Twitter, LinkedIn, and Dropbox, and more specialized services like Match.com or Yelp. This has been described as "The Subscription Economy" and brings out the full richness of the transition from Goods-Dominant Logic to Service-Dominant Logic. Companies are already realizing that this is a fundamental shift in how they do business, manage operations, and do financial accounting. Subscription commerce refocuses the objective, to not just seek cash from transactions, but to seek renewal. That leads to ongoing revenue streams that can be grown, in terms of frequency, add-ons, usage, and upgrades. That, in turn, leads to much greater revenue opportunity, and involves changes (and ongoing adaptation) in product and pricing strategy, customer subscription management, billing and payments, and analytics.

   FairPay cycles map directly to the periodic cycles of subscriptions, with services offered for defined intervals of time, and pricing backward on the experience of each completed interval, and extended forward to additional intervals. FairPay can be used to set prices for each interval as a cycle, or in simplified forms over some number of intervals treated together as a single FairPay pricing cycle.

We will explore subscription uses for journalism (in greatest detail, as exemplary), music, and TV/video.

2. *Discrete item sales (in ongoing relationships, such as by aggregators).* Examples include Amazon, iTunes, and the like, and software app stores, as well as other distributors of music, games, apps, and e-books. (We will also explore non-digital item-oriented uses.)

FairPay can be effective here as well, by managing FairPay offers as relating to bundles of items (as opposed to intervals of access). For example, it could be applied to customer-selected bundles (any desired selection) of 5 or 10 songs, or albums, or e-books, or software apps. The pricing backward is done for each such bundle (with feedback on individual items as desired), and it is then extended forward to offer additional bundles. (More in the next section.)

To summarize likely product/service categories a bit more specifically, these include:

- Anything with low marginal cost
  - Long-tail of content—low-popularity products (expand market/gain revenue)
  - Short-head of content—high-popularity products (expand market/gain revenue)
- Digital content/products/services (by item or by subscription)
  - News/information/magazines
  - Video
  - Music
  - Games
  - E-Books
  - Apps/Software
  - Other Digital Services
- Real products/services (especially experience goods)
  - Low marginal cost (primary product or extras/support)
  - Sampling/trials/coupons/promotions (e.g., Groupon)
  - Perishable excess (e.g., hotels, transport, performances)
  - Costly goods—with a minimum price floor + FairPay bonus

In general, FairPay is especially well suited where the following apply:

- Experience goods/services, which are hard to predict the value of until they are actually experienced by the particular customer.
- Items with low marginal cost, where the cost of learning whether a given customer will price fairly is low. This is typical of most digital products/services (those that are not resource-intensive). It also applies to non-digital items that are perishable (like hotel rooms or restaurant seatings) and in cases of special promotions (like a Groupon coupon business).
- Costly goods/services are a bit more challenging, but there seems to be interesting potential in setting a minimum "floor" price (paid up-front) to cover variable costs, and then a post-priced bonus to provide a fair profit after the value is fully known (such as for a service like Etsy).
- Appreciative customers and "deserving" sellers/creators. Obviously fairness and generosity in pricing will be highest from customers who appreciate what they are getting and feel that the supplier merits their support to sustain that. This gets to the idea of "patronship" as discussed in some of the following examples, such as for journalism and the arts, and for socially conscious companies. And, of course, such an appeal is especially relevant to nonprofit organizations.
- Any of these in a secondary line of business—even for businesses in which the primary product/service may not be well suited. These may include product support and ancillary services.

And keep in mind that all of these markets can be served by FairPay as a platform business (Pricing as a Service), with additional leverage and economies of scale, as discussed in Chapter 13.

Item-Oriented Versus Subscription Purchases

As we look at specific industries in the following sections, we encounter a mix of subscription-oriented sales and item-oriented sales. The fundamentals are largely the same, but some details vary. A given business may have some of each. We introduced the case of subscription in Chapter 4—here we complement that with a brief look at item sales.

This could be any kind of item: music, games, news stories, or even physical items. More detail, including aspects related to an aggregator that sells items for many independent providers, is provided for the example of an app store in Chapter 10.

The FairPay process for an item-oriented business (such as an app store) can be quite simple:

- The store offers to let buyers try a small number of FairPay-eligible items on a FairPay basis, with the understanding that the buyer can try the items for a time, and *then* set whatever price they consider fair. The full FairPay process would be explained in detail up-front, so buyers understand that future FairPay offers will depend on what reputation they develop for paying fairly.
- The buyer tries the items, then sets prices, and can indicate why they paid what they did. For example, a buyer might explain that they were disappointed in a product if that is why they decided to pay little or nothing for it. (Of course they can also say they love it, or love the band/developer, and want to pay especially well.) A suggested price for each item might be provided for guidance.
- The store then assesses the prices paid, and the reasons, and decides whether to offer that buyer more items on the same FairPay basis. Criteria might include consideration of item-specific suggested prices, and the prices set by other FairPay buyers.
  - Those who pay well will get a continuing stream of further FairPay offers (as long as they continue to pay reasonably well). Those who pay well for some, and explain why not for others, might also get some further offers (effectively on a probationary basis), until it is determined by the store that they either do or do not pay fairly—whether for particular product categories, or in general.

- ○ Those judged by the store to generally not pay at an acceptable level can be cut off from further FairPay offers (in general, or by category), and restricted to conventional, set-price sales (at least for some time, possibly extending a second chance to try FairPay sometime in the future).
- The cycle continues, based on these evolving FairPay reputations. The longer this process runs, the more meaningful the FairPay fairness reputations of the buyers, and the better able the store and developers are to manage revenue and risk, by controlling what offers are made to which buyers.

Behavioral Engineering, Choice Architectures, and Dialogs About Value

Here is a brief summary of the key principles. Later chapters expand on how this applies in specific industries, and review the behavioral economics and game theory principles of why and how this can be effective.

FairPay provides an adaptive learning engine that enables each customer to find a pricing style that works for him and for the seller. Customers who adapt to this new dynamic can find a new freedom to get what they want at a price that they agree is fair. Those who value the product and have willingness and ability to pay will be offered the world. Those who see less value and are willing and able to pay less will still get most of what they want, again at a price they agree is fair. Those who repeatedly refuse to pay fairly enough to satisfy the seller will get cut off from FairPay offers. (They may instead be given the option to buy at the full set price.)

FairPay sellers build real relationships with individual customers in which the customer feels understood and respected. These "dialogs about value" focus on the value of the product, the service, and larger social values that matter to the customer. Sellers who convince customers that they not only produce good products, but are also good partners and good corporate citizens, can draw on communal norms of behavior to entice generous "premium" pricing,

Sellers might restrict the FairPay offers that they extend to new customers who lack established FairPay reputations. They might even restrict them to items and quantities that would otherwise be free trials (much as with freemium pricing), so that their risk is small. Only after the customer establishes a history of paying fairly will the seller continue to make FairPay offers for larger quantities or more premium items. *The benefits to the customer of not paying will be limited and short-lived. The benefits of paying fairly will continue and grow.*

Sellers can be expected to make these consequences clear when they first extend an offer to sell on a FairPay basis. The product/service is not offered as "free," nor as simple PWYW, but as *Fair PWYW*, or perhaps better put as *Pay What You Think Fair*—essentially on trial, on approval, and on evaluation. Sellers would make it clear that zero is "acceptable" (with regard to reputation and future consequences) only if that is arguably fair. Such cases of reasonable fairness in setting a zero price might include cases in which the customer gives a reason why there is little or no realized value to the customer (much as is often required for returns)—or where only very low quantities are sampled (which might be accepted as a customer-directed form of free sampling).

Game-Based Marketing and Loyalty Programs

One potentially important level of sophistication in choice architectures that is only touched on here is gamification. Given the nature of FairPay as a repeated game, adding elements to more directly gamify the customer journey might be very popular and effective for some customers. Such methods have become a popular tool in varied aspects of e-commerce and loyalty programs.

Well-designed choice architectures are essential to managing Fair-Pay—to encourage open and frank dialogs about value, and to help motivate generous pricing. Some customers can be stimulated by adding explicit gamification elements that offer recognition and competitive status, such as points, levels, badges, challenges and rewards. These can be focused within relationships with individual customers, or can create open competition among customers who gain status relative to other customers on leaderboards or by getting other visible rewards such as badges that signify their generosity and cooperative engagement.

FairPay pricing of loyalty program rewards in the currency of miles or points is also an important opportunity, and an interesting place to consider early trials. Current loyalty programs for credit card usage, travel services like airline mileage programs, and for other services often provide points that can be redeemed for rewards. Why not allow reward prices in points to be set using FairPay? What better way to enhance the loyalty of your best customers by extending them that special FairPay privilege?

Transparency, "Trust but Verify," and Context

The quest for win–win is a fundamental change of mindset from the zero-sum mentality that pervades much of modern commerce. Businesses are very secretive as to their pricing strategies, how they discriminate and segment markets, what their costs are, what their profit margins are, and the why of all that. Consumers play the counter game of seeking bargains and trading "intelligence" (strategies, discount codes, and the like). We even seek ombudsmen to balance the most extreme power inequities—the *New York Times* has a column called "The Haggler," that champions abused consumers.

For the cooperative dialog of FairPay to be effective in creating win–win relationships, we must shift toward levels of transparency and trust that push the boundaries of current commercial relationships. That may cause fear and loathing for businesses more used to trying to put things over on their customers and feeling that customers cannot be trusted. (I am reminded of the War Room scene in *Dr. Strangelove*, as the Soviet ambassador enters.) Later chapters dig into these issues of customer-hostile value propositions and the behavioral economic and psychological principles behind FairPay, but for now, some brief comments.

- On transparency, companies are realizing that they do better when customers trust them to provide real value and not play deceitful games against them. Mobile phone and cable TV companies are pulling back from notorious extremes of customer-hostility. Apparel company Everlane is extolling its transparency about sourcing, costs, and profits. FairPay builds on these directions to make co-creation of value a more truly cooperative effort.

- On trust, people question how customers can be trusted to set fair prices and not lie in their dialogs about value. Here the idea of "trust but verify" is relevant. As noted earlier, Big Data about how customers use products and services is providing very rich data about consumption and implicit metrics of value (a Cloud of Value). It will be increasingly easy to validate what customers say in their dialogs about value against the hard data on what they actually did. If you quit a book or a song a short time into it, that would support a claim that you did not find it valuable. If you read a book through in successive long sittings, or played a song 20 times in a month, such a claim would clearly be very dubious.

Price Discrimination Can Be Good!

Transparency can enhance the viability of dynamic pricing and the more win–win forms of price discrimination applied in FairPay. (Some interesting references are at FPZLink.)

Dynamic pricing is theoretically optimal, but has been perceived as inequitable in consumer markets, and price discrimination is almost a dirty word (actually illegal in some situations). Amazon experimented with price discrimination in its early days, and backed off after negative reactions, but there are occasional reports that other vendors discriminate by location. Uber's "surge-pricing" policies have now made this a hot topic again.

The real problem is one that can largely be fixed in a "postmodern" economy. The problem with dynamic pricing is that it is set unilaterally by the seller, and imposed on the customer on a "take it or leave it" basis (if not hidden completely). But, still, discrimination is economically optimal. That is why it is widely used in the hotel, airline, and car rental businesses. In those industries customers have learned to live with it—but still with considerable resentment. *The way to make price discrimination acceptable to customers is to involve them in the pricing decision.*

That is one of the key features of FairPay. Applying FairPay's long-term relationship view, customers have significant participation in pricing, and can be asked by sellers to include a dynamic premium if it is for good reason—*but they can decide just how extreme that premium should be.* Sellers get to determine if the customer is generally being fair about that, and continue to allow FairPay pricing in the future to those who are.

Remember, it is abundance, not scarcity, that FairPay thrives on. The more tractable form of discrimination is when the premium is not to ration scarce supply, but to ration share of wallet where replication is free—to reflect cases where a customer gets higher value or has higher ability to pay. It is much harder to justify being indignant about unfairness in such cases, especially when it is tied to contributing a fair share toward sustaining creation of new services that are valued.

Another factor in customer acceptance is predictability. This is really a problem of unpleasant surprises, and price changes that seem unfair. The perceived unfairness of dynamic prices and discrimination, such as with the Uber's New Year's surge, or for snow shovels or flashlights after a storm, is the "unfair" external imposition of higher prices. Here again, when the customer gets to opt in to the level of dynamic premium, that changes it to a fair and equitable process.

Which brings us back to transparency. Transparency leads to a deeper level of consumer understanding that makes it easier to justify price discrepancies that might otherwise seem unfair. What if one customer talks to another and learns he has gotten a very different price for an item?

- FairPay increases both transparency and context-dependency. If two customers find that they have very different prices for "similar" content under FairPay, such as for music, it will become apparent that they are comparing different amounts of usage, at different times, different genre mixes, different levels of advertising, different levels of playlist control, different ability to pay, different satisfaction levels, and many other disparities in usage context and value (and sellers can highlight such factors).

- It will be apparent that they are comparing apples and oranges, and that a higher price corresponds to higher value received, which is justified and fair—and that the customer has agreed to that without being a chump.

Thus "discrimination" can be good—when done within reason, at agreed-upon levels, based on mutually understood reasons.

CHAPTER 8

Case Study: Journalism, Newspapers, Magazines, Video

This chapter provides the most in-depth case study of FairPay and how it changes the game in a particular business. Journalism is particularly fertile ground, and deserves review even if your interests are elsewhere. We refer to journalism broadly, to include newspapers, magazines, and Web content, including video. The important case of entertainment video, including TV and movies, is addressed at the end of this chapter. The next chapters cover other industries as variations on themes that are addressed in more depth here. (See more at FPZLink.)

Journalism is one of the industries most disrupted by digital technologies (Kaiser 2014). Classifieds died first, and then free distribution of news on the Web led many consumers to think all news should be free. Advertising was hoped to be the sustaining revenue source, but ad revenues have plummeted as changes in technology and ad-blockers have put that in serious doubt.

Journalism has nearly all of the attributes for a promising application of FairPay. News, especially investigative journalism, is costly to create, but nearly free to distribute. It is an experience good, with a value that varies widely depending on who is reading it, when, and for what purpose. The seller is deserving, if providing quality journalism that readers appreciate and may feel a moral imperative to help sustain—the idea of patronship.

To set the stage, let's review what people have been saying about the challenges of journalism in the digital era—beginning with some very Internet-savvy billionaires who have decided to jump in to help.

Jeff Bezos and *The Washington Post*—"Why Should I Pay You?"

Jeff Bezos's purchase of the *Post* in 2013 drew wide attention. At the time he made some interesting points in an interview (Farhi 2013):

> The Post is famous for its investigative journalism. It pours energy and investment and sweat and dollars into uncovering important stories. And then a bunch of Web sites summarize that [work] in about four minutes and readers can access that news for free. One question is, how do you make a living in that kind of environment? If you can't, it's difficult to put the right resources behind it. … Even behind a paywall [digital subscription], Web sites can summarize your work and make it available for free. From a reader point of view, the reader has to ask, "Why should I pay you for all that journalistic effort when I can get it for 'free' from another site?"

"Why should I pay you?" is the central dilemma of Internet content, and exactly the question the FairPay process is designed to answer. There is no one simple answer, but I suggest this general shape for an answer:

- *We ask you to pay only what you think fair for the value we provide you—isn't that fair?* The quality journalism we provide is expensive to produce, and if people like you who value it do not pay a fair price, how can we continue to provide it?
- *We will treat you as an individual patron—we will listen carefully to what you want, and you will get our best efforts to produce and deliver it to you.*

There is no one simple answer—but *FairPay offers a reasonably simple process for seeking the answer* in all its complexity, by fully applying the one-to-one power of the Internet:

- The answer is an individual one. It will vary from person to person, from day to day.
- Finding that answer requires an ongoing, individualized process.
- It also requires individualized pricing, a concept that is challenging as well.

This is a problem that was made difficult by the Internet, as Bezos observes, but it is also a problem that can now be solved using methods enabled by the Internet.

So *"Why should I pay?"—The essence of the FairPay process is to undertake deep, computer-assisted dialogs with the reader on just that question:*

- The answer must be individualized to pin down what value *The Post* actually delivers to me.
- It must structure a dialog to learn what I think *The Post* is worth to me—and to help *frame* my evaluation to fully appreciate the value I receive.
- It must close the loop to drive toward a fair exchange between me and *The Post* over time.
- The first cycles of this dialog may give poor results, but with good feedback and direction, this can drive an emergent process that delivers value, sets prices for that value, and converges toward a fair value exchange.

In his letter to *Post* employees (Bezos 2013), *Bezos said "There is no map"—but I suggest that the FairPay process provides a map*—it may be crude and in need of corrections, like early maps of "the new world" but, like them, it is good enough to start a journey in the right general direction, even if that journey may take some unexpected pivots.

Bezos emphasizes that there is a need for experimentation and patience—FairPay offers *a structured process for ongoing experimentation* that can be expected to move toward convergence, and to provide data to shed light on any rough spots so the process can be altered to work even better. Think of it as an adaptive value discovery engine.

FairPay centers on the idea of customers as patrons who have only to be motivated. It provides a mechanism for them to be patrons of journalism. (It works similarly for patrons of books, music, video, apps, and other digital offerings.)

The essence of FairPay is in the workings of this engine:

- To view transactions not as ends in themselves, but as steps in a process that builds a relationship based on fair value exchange;

- To let you learn and adapt, to provide what your patrons value;
- To let the patrons learn pay according to the value they perceive, and to be fair about that;
- To guide these dynamics, to motivate both the patrons to pay a fair price, and your efforts to seek to delight them.

FairPay draws on several important enablers:

- *Modern behavioral economics* that shows that people are not heartless profit maximizers, but can be motivated by a sense of fairness and related aspects of reciprocity, altruism, and self-image to pay more than they have to (share their "value surplus"), when given a good reason. Supporting the quality journalism of *The Post*, for my own benefit, for the common good, and out of fairness, is just such a reason—if given in terms that are specifically relevant to me and responsive to my concerns. *Think of me as a patron, and make me want to be a patron.*
- *Computer-assisted dialog*, and the growing ease of use and power of such dialogs to inform the process of understanding what I value, and to help me to recognize what value I have received. *Engage me as a patron and show that you understand what I care about.*
- *Predictive analytics* that can help *The Post* to shape both the service it offers me and the dialog it has with me in a way that gives me what I really care about, and makes me want to pay a fair price for it. *I will be a patron if I feel what I patronize is worthwhile and respects my desires.*

How much should I pay? FairPay treats that as a matter for dialog. Only I can determine what I value, and what price I think fair for it. FairPay lets me pay what I think fair. ... But it does not stop there.

Why should I pay fairly? FairPay enables *The Post* to suggest what I should pay, track what I do pay, understand why I think my price is fair, and tell me whether they agree it is fair. All of this is specific to what I read, how often, how much, for how long; whether I read it for business or pleasure; how affluent I am; and many other details. *The*

Post can measure and report that to me, consider what I say about the value I perceive, and factor that into their suggested price. They can tell me that they think I am being unfair, and limit what they offer me, or they can tell me that I am being generous and enrich what they offer me. If *The Post* plays this game well (mostly carrot, a little bit of stick), they can give me what I value, and motivate me to pay a fair price for it.

These enablers and this value discovery engine inform a new invisible hand (my invisible handshake), one that can entice readers to happily pay a fair price for the content they consume. It gives the reader the power to set a price they are comfortable with, but gives the publisher the power to nudge that to a level the publisher is also comfortable with over time (or to cut back on what is offered).

That new dynamic balances my goals and *The Post*'s. *The Post* can gamble on my fairness for a time, to see if am willing to be a patron. (Doing so costs them almost nothing.) If not, it can leave me to deal with a conventional paywall subscription, or to fend for myself. If I am willing to be a patron, *The Post* can serve me at whatever level I justify that I am paying fairly for.

This fits perfectly with the guidelines Bezos outlined in his letter to Post employees:

"We will need to invent ..."

... this map is both an invention and a framework for continuing invention.

"... which means we will need to experiment"

... FairPay is a method for ongoing experimentation in the form of structured dialog with readers, for dynamically learning what they value, at what price, and for guiding the Post's adaptation to provide it.

"Our touchstone will be readers, understanding what they care about ... and working backwards from there"

... that is the touchstone of FairPay, turning the invisible hand to drive just that, in a new kind of emergent pricing process.

More Billionaire Patrons

Pierre Omidyar, founder of eBay, also considered buying *The Washington Post*, but revealed in his blog (Omidyar 2013) that he decided instead to actively participate in developing an entirely new media platform intended to support and empower independent journalists.

In tune with Bezos, Omidyar points to the primacy of customer relationships in e-commerce (in his interview by David Carr [2013]):

> Technologists understand our users and break down how user engagement increases from somebody that maybe just tries your product once and then goes away, to a different kind of person that progressively gets more and more engaged and then becomes just totally locked into your product. That's something people in Silicon Valley spend a ton of time analyzing, working on and thinking about.

FairPay integrates engagement directly into the value exchange process.

Omidyar said (to Jay Rosen, [Rosen 2013]) he wants to run his venture as "a company, not a charity." That means generating a revenue stream (presumably from readers, not advertisers). Rosen describes this as "the personal franchise model." The ability to *engage readers to serve as patrons* is essential to that.

FairPay naturally integrates the reader's evaluation of a journalist's value directly into the pricing process. It engages the reader in ongoing "dialogs about value" on how the reader values the work of each journalist over the course of their relationship. Readers intuitively recognize many dimensions of value, and the dialog can easily be structured to elicit pricing that factors in this judgment with regard to such dimensions as quality, style, investigation, reader value, and social value.

With FairPay, an Omidyar media platform can get direct feedback from each reader on the perceived value of each article, the body of work by that journalist, and the media service as a whole.

- This can be directly linked to compensation for each journalist, thus increasing engagement and the quality of the relationship on both sides.

- Readers will know that a significant portion of their payments go to the journalists, and that their feedback bears directly on how journalists are paid (and what investigations are funded).
- Conversely, journalists will be motivated to create a body of work that readers recognize as valuable by voting for them with their wallets.

This gets to the issue of "Creating Shared Value," as is discussed later. FairPay is uniquely focused on creating the multidimensional dialogs on value that are needed to turn readers into patrons of important journalism. It not only supports the journalistic effort, but guides it to the tasks that the reader/patrons consider important.

- It builds a deep relationship with readers that can feed directly into the key editorial processes that determine which journalists to support, in what investigations, and how they are paid.
- It builds a value discovery engine into the heart of the media platform, to drive it toward work that is good and important, and to get readers engaged as patrons who pay for that, both for themselves and for the common good.

And given a model in which (as Rosen reports) "all proceeds ... will be reinvested in journalism," readers can be strongly motivated to be generous patrons. Omidyar is quoted as saying he started eBay on the premise that "people are basically good." Modern behavioral economics demonstrates that his faith is well founded. FairPay offers a way to apply that virtue to support a wide range of valued services, including quality journalism. In doing that, it leads to the answer to Jeff Bezos's central question: "Why should I pay you."

Another billionaire patron of Journalism is John Henry, who purchased the *Boston Globe*, also in 2013. In a letter to the *Globe* (Henry 2013), he said he recognized that "journalism's business model had become fundamentally flawed. Readers were flocking from the papers to the Internet, consuming expensive journalism for free. On the advertising front, print dollars were giving way to digital dimes. I decided that the challenges were too difficult, so I moved on. Or, I should say, I tried to move on." He went on to say "My every intention is to push the kind of boldness and investment that will make the *Globe* a laboratory for major newspapers across the country."

So with this recognition of the broken business models of journalism, and the need to experiment, how can we break through—from just doing things right, to doing the right thing? And how can we do it in a way that does not depend on a few public-spirited billionaires? Journalism is too important to be left to the billionaires.

Progress Toward a "Subscription Economy"

Of course there has been progress, not just from the billionaires. Major players have been moving from free to freemium combinations of limited free access (for some small number of articles per month), with a "paywall" requiring paid subscriptions for more access. Such "soft" or "metered" pay-walls are a simple but major improvement over the "hard" paywalls of the past, still used by many publications, that require a paid, unlimited-access subscription to read even a single article. Talk about "customer-hostile" value propositions! (the subject of Chapter 18). *The New York Times* has committed to this (as nicely described by Carr [2010]), and continues to report gradual progress—a 2015 statement reports reaching $400 million in revenues and the objective of reaching $800 million by 2020.

Zuora.com, a provider of subscription platform "Software as a Service" has been a strong advocate of the transition to what it calls *The Subscription Economy.* (This is related to the broader trend to more flexible exchange of services, including the "sharing economy" of Uber, ZipCar, AriBnB, and the like.) Zuora president Tien Tzuo, describes current trends as "Paywall 2.0," and says "focusing on customers is the only way to win." (Tzuo 2012)

This is an excellent foundation for FairPay as the next step—which I am calling Paywall 3.0. Zuora is right about Paywall 2.0, and FairPay builds on that to deepen—and center on—the customer relationship.

The first rule of Paywall 3.0 is that there is no paywall—there is a FairPay Zone in which readers may pay or not, and publishers decide case by case, and month by month, on what basis to maintain the relationship with each reader. This goes way beyond "soft" and "porous" paywalls and brings in aspects of a membership model (as expanded on later in this chapter).

As noted by Tzuo,

> ... as the demise of Variety shows, paywalls are not enough. That's because it's never been just about the paywall—it's about publishers viewing readers not as anonymous demographic statistics to sell to advertisers, but as customers who are willing to pay for something of value. In this changing customer-centric world, media and publishing companies need to adopt a more data-driven approach to understanding customers, design bundles and pricing plans that meet their needs, and strengthen their relationships with customers to ensure a they'll keep coming back for more. Let's call it Paywall 2.0 ...

> Now starts the hard road to recovery. And that recovery will come from a truly customer-centric approach. It is about building customer relationships, finding ways to build loyalty, having a range of offerings from free to paid-for that make sense ...

> Paywall 1.0 was a good start, but isn't enough. Publishers need to move towards the second iteration ...

> I firmly believe we live in a world where success is not about how many products you ship. It's about how strong your customer relationships are, and how well you are monetising those relationships.

Similar directions are suggested by Piano, which now owns Press+, a pioneering paywall platform originally launched as Journalism Online. They report:

> Piano's industry-leading VX software is based on a value exchange model that uses big data to segment audience and present user's different monetization options based on their individual profiles. Further the company now offers advanced data and CRM capabilities to help content companies identify and segment their audience, enabling business models targeted to the individual user. The platform integrates easily alongside existing advertising solutions,

allowing clients to optimize their mix of paid and ad-supported media. (Piano 2015)

These are all steps in the right direction. Many who seek to preserve serious journalism, who believe that we need more than clickbait and the uncritical crowdsourcing of news, have been scrambling—and they are actually finding many ways to get revenue (as summarized later in this chapter). Nevertheless, it is hard to have conviction that even the best of them can be sufficient—they fall far short of the change in value propositions that is really needed. FairPay is fully compatible with these trends, and builds on them. (In fact Zuora has expressed an interest in adding FairPay into their offering, as an alternative approach to pricing that their clients can apply as an option.) The next section looks closer at how FairPay fits in.

Patronizing Journalism—Beyond Paywalls, Meters, and Membership

These are very turbulent times for journalism. But back to Peter Drucker, *what we need is a new logic.* FairPay is a new logic that draws synergy from all relevant revenue streams, in a way that leverages digital, to radically transform the relationship of journalists with their audiences.

Why be a customer? Why pay? The only way for journalism to survive in this new century is to refocus on a new logic for patronship—getting readers to patronize content providers in the fullest sense: "to give money or support to." To find sustainable business models for journalism in a digital world, we must figure out how to find patrons (in this broad sense), and how to work with them so they are happy to contribute at sustainable levels.

Newspapers, magazines, and news video services are struggling to find a logic that works. Paywalls, "soft" "metered" paywalls (a form of freemium), have been adopted by many publishers as a primary model (but still avoided by many others). They seem to be working just marginally, even in the best of cases. But we have been looking at the trees, not seeing that there can be a new kind of forest.

- Paywalls (soft or not) treat customers as faceless, undifferentiated cattle to be herded and milked. There is no invitation to be a patron, no personalization of the value proposition, even though individuals vary immensely in how they value and consume journalism. How can a single price possibly be right for all subscribers?

- Premium level subscriptions (such as *Times Insider*) have emerged (with apparently limited success) as a supplementary strategy to try to get the most loyal patrons to pay more, based on the realization that some of them can be enticed to do so. But here too, value propositions are not customized.

- Patronship at the high end has always been a key support for journalism, from the rich owners of the past, to Bezos, Henry, and Omidyar today. That is a nice contribution but it seems a shaky foundation for something so important to the public— something that should be answerable only to its public.

- Crowdfunding and tipjars (microdonations) seek to move patronship to a wider base, but that seems fragmented, decoupled from operations, and very limited as well.

- Membership has become the latest hot topic (subject of a CUNY/Tow-Knight conference in 2015 that I attended). This gets much closer to the core ideas of patronship. These efforts are a big step toward recognizing the need for more flexible targeting of value propositions, and addressing the many different kinds of value that can be exchanged. This can include a very wide spectrum of offers to the audience(s)— from added features, access to journalists, events, and bling, to pure contribution (drawing on the model of public radio and TV memberships). It also begins to recognize that value also flows *from* customers *to* providers of journalism, the "reverse meter" (Jarvis 2011). It was evident at the conference that membership is a rich and promising area, already generating some success, but how to manage this almost too-rich variety of value propositions is a challenge.

- This is not to forget that advertising remains an important source of revenue, even if increasingly limited. Many of the audience would pay to reduce that burden—and some might accept more (to get more value or lower prices—another reverse meter). But, again, there is little customization of such value propositions. (See the ad-blocking discussion in Chapter 18.)

The Bigger Picture

Journalists have targeted a growing variety of revenue sources, but none a silver bullet. Where is the overarching synergy? What is tomorrow's logic?

The answer is to link this rich constellation of value propositions into a coherent, adaptive process—one that seeks to find the right combination of value propositions for each individual, match them to their willingness to pay, and serve them in a customized bundle—in a cooperative way that makes every regular customer into a true patron. If journalism has value, shouldn't those who are served by it recognize that value, and pay to sustain it? (As has often been observed, "if you are not the customer, you are the product.")

That can be done in many ways, and many are being tried and improved on, but I suggest the most effective way to apply the best methods in concert will be by drawing them into the FairPay architecture. This architecture shapes a platform for applying all of the best methods in unison, to cooperatively find the right value proposition (and the right price) for each patron.

Re-Engineering the Value Proposition of Journalism for the Digital Era

The big picture idea is that FairPay refocuses journalism businesses on their relationship with their individual audience members—with all the tools of the digital era—to center on co-designing personalized, win–win value propositions. It builds this relationship on a cooperative understanding of individualized value that integrates all of the relevant elements on both sides of the value exchange. It seeks to enable a holistic view of value (and revenue)—basic subscriptions, premiums, membership options, perks, and any other kinds of offers, over all aspects of the value exchange.

From the provider to the customer, FairPay focuses on the total value of all kinds, as actually delivered to each particular customer—the value-in-use for exactly what is consumed and how (what items, how many, how intensely), including content, membership perks, and so on—the value of that experience and potentially even the outcomes that result (enjoyment, appreciation, and the results enabled—did our advice improve your health or you stock market returns?). This can also include "soft" values, such as

- Service and support;
- Participation, listening, and responsiveness (comments, access to the journalists);
- Events and merchandise; and
- The social value of investigative journalism, community services, and good corporate citizenship.

From the customer to the provider, FairPay considers not just monetary payments (subscription or membership fees, or pay-per-use), but other currencies. Thus it factors in credits (the "reverse meter") for

- Attention to advertising (including the possibility of customized levels of ad loads);
- Personal data that can be used or sold (again with possible customization);
- The value of user-generated content;
- The value of viral promotion and leads; and
- Volunteer-provided services to the publisher.

As my value-pricing demon would tell us, an ideal economic exchange must fully consider all of these aspects of value, and determine how to balance the exchange in a way that fairly shared the "economic surplus" (of value over cost) between the provider and the customer. As we have seen, this is not just an economic ideal, but FairPay provides a practical process for getting customers and providers to cooperate in approximating that ideal—an adaptive engine for jointly evaluating the value actually received, and sharing fairly in the surplus.

FairPay re-engineers how the providers of journalism interact with their audience members to deal with value, compensation, and sustainability, and creates a new balance of power. It recognizes that journalism co-creates value with its audience(s), and applies an adaptive method of co-pricing that (1) gives audience members the power to pay commensurate with the value they perceive and can afford, while (2) retaining the power for providers to demand that be done fairly and sustainably.

As explained in other sections, this approach draws support from a number of emerging areas of theory:

- Marketing theory: Journalism is recognized as being not a product but a service—and services involve not a unidirectional transfer of value from a producer to a customer, but a joint co-creation of value.
- Behavioral economics and game theory: Recent behavioral economics findings show that people will pay voluntarily for services, if asked in the right way, and game theory shows how repeated games can drive cooperation.
- Value-based pricing: There has been notable success with "value-based" pricing (or "performance-based" or "outcomes-based" models) for pricing industrial equipment and services. FairPay points to how a lightweight, heuristic variation on that theme can work for computer-mediated mass consumer markets.

Why Take the Risk?

Journalism is in a downward spiral, with a shrinking market of people willing to pay for it, at least on current terms. FairPay brings a robust and coherent strategy that applies across the spectrum of patronship:

- *For the Long Tail of Customers*, FairPay promises to make it more affordable for the huge population of people who might pay something, but do not pay at all now because they will not pay as much as paywalls demand. FairPay's customized pricing can adapt to the lower, but still profitable, payments of the large population who consume lightly.
- *For the Tall head of Customers*, FairPay also promises to capture a larger "share of wallet" of those who are already paying. Unlike the complex and confusing value propositions of

membership and set-price premium subscriptions, FairPay
can tailor rich value propositions to the desires of each patron,
especially those willing to pay to get what they really want,
not just some arbitrary, standard bundle.

The result is a holistic view of value propositions, and how monetary payments fit in with other aspects of value, that enables the engine
to individually manage a win–win relationship over time. It motivates a
very wide range of customers of journalism to act as patrons, who provide an individualized mixture of money and other currencies of value
that are a fair and sustainable exchange for what the customer uses and
values. It works as an adaptive, emergent process that identifies desired
value propositions, delivers on them, tracks the results, and sets prices
that patrons accept as fair and are happy to pay. Subscriptions, premiums, membership, and patronship fit together into an integrated engine
of value creation and exchange, one that patrons can understand and fully
buy into. This goes beyond the old invisible hand—which is no longer
operative for digital services—to the more collaborative balance of an
invisible handshake.

The bottom line is that FairPay promises to enable sales to a much
larger market for much more profit. Some will pay more than now and
some less—average revenue per subscriber may decrease, but the larger
number of subscribers can more than compensate. And for partially
ad-supported businesses, more subscribers also means more ad revenue.

While FairPay is very much aligned with the latest thinking in marketing and e-commerce, applying something so unconventional is not
without risk. Established businesses will want to test FairPay first at the
margins, in limited, controlled trials. This can be done in many areas,
including premium tiers, acquisition offers, and retention offers (see
Chapter 7). Even if it does not work exactly as expected, FairPay points
us in the right direction—that of *constantly learning about realized value
propositions and adapting to what each individual patron wants and values
at any given time*.

Trying it will lead to learning how to do it right—how much power
to give to your patrons, in what way. *Really listening to our customers* is
now something that technology not only greatly facilitates, but requires

us to do very well. It is not optional, something that can be neglected—it is now central to the co-creation of journalism—and the business of journalism.

News Aggregators and FairPay

Of course, few newspapers or other news businesses have the critical mass of readership of the *Times* or even the *Globe*. Aggregation can be valuable to make it easy for customers to access journalism from varied sources. Blendle has gotten much recent attention, and the proposal for The Internet Trust Exchange also seems promising. These approaches generally rely on micropayments to address varying levels of usage. Micropayments have had a troubled history (as Clay Shirky summarized long ago [2000]), but they do partially address the challenge of linking price to value when usage varies widely.

FairPay is very applicable to use by aggregators, and it addresses the problems of micropayments directly, so that customers need not fear the ticking meter, as explained in the sections on "post-bundling" and on "all you can eat" (AYCE) subscriptions. Post-bundling builds in volume discounts after the fact. And when done using FairPay, these post-bundling volume discounts are soft and forgiving suggestions that are not binding, so customers need have little anxiety about usage.

Simple post-bundling can be done even without the more radical aspects of FairPay—if we do nothing more than apply pre-set discount rates from a provider-specified discount schedule, there is still a significant benefit. Why should my incremental cost for one more article be very low (actually zero) if I am an average subscriber on an unlimited usage subscription plan, but high if I have the same activity level using a micropayment system? The incremental charge for an added article should be very small (once beyond some minimal level of volume). The reason consumers hate micropayments is this relentlessly unforgiving meter—if we cannot make the meter go away, we must at least make it tick more softly and be more forgiving. (Blendle does take one small but smart step in the direction of customer participation, by making it very easy to demand an instant refund if not satisfied with an article—more at FPZLink.)

Entertainment Video, TV, and Movies

To segue from journalism, entertainment video is another major content industry facing digital disruption. How FairPay applies to it can be understood as very similar to the examples given here for journalism, and for music and games, especially as related to aggregators. We add discussion of the issues of TV channel bundling in Chapter 18 (and more at FPZLink).

CHAPTER 9

Variations: Music (and Games)

Much as described for journalism, the economics of the music business also remain highly problematic. The revenue pie for recorded music is a fraction of what it once was, and artists/creators complain that they are seeing only crumbs out of what little remains. At the same time music is more available—and artists are closer to their fans—than ever. The problem is that most listeners pay little, if at all. In fact, music was the first major content industry to face serious disruption by digital ("Napsterization").

Music could benefit greatly from FairPay, but the complex, century-old supply chain of the mainstream music business makes change difficult. The independent music business might be the easiest place to start.

The video/computer games business has many similarities to music in terms of industry structure, with independent artists/creators/developers, who work with studios/labels, and often sell through distributors, so much of this discussion applies to games as well—and the good news is that industry practice is less entrenched. (More on both is at FPZLink.)

Continuing Turmoil

The music business has been turned upside down by the challenges of Internet distribution and related piracy, to the point that the prominent band Radiohead offered its 2007 album for download on a pay what you want (PWYW) basis (Pareles 2007). While a reported 60 percent of downloaders did not pay at all, 40 percent did (paying an average of $8.05 in the United States and $4.64 elsewhere), enough to make that experiment modestly successful, and that led to similar offers by other groups.

Even though the crisis has eased a bit, as first iTunes, and later subscription services such as Pandora and Spotify, are convincing many people to pay something, business models remain besieged. The 2016 Global Music Report (IFPI 2016) refers to "a value gap"

> The value gap is about the gross mismatch between music being enjoyed by consumers and the revenues being returned to the music community. Today, music consumption is exploding, driven by streaming services and in particular by the rapidly-growing use of user upload platforms such as YouTube.

The report lists the number of users paying for music subscription services as 68 million, compared to 900 million using free or ad-supported services. Clearly any strategy that can get a reasonable fraction of those listeners to pay has very large potential.

Radical models of disintermediation, with artists/creators (performers and songwriters) going directly to fans and even selling on a PWYW basis, have shown that we are ripe for new ideas, but none have yet proven broadly workable. There continue to be numerous pleas for new business models for music. Sounds like a job for FairPay!

Revisiting the Economics—The Size of the Pie—and the Portion of the Pie

The core problem is that the value and the economically efficient price for recorded music is not well captured by any conventional model. Primary criteria are:

1. A fair price to the listener based on value received
2. A fair portion to the artists/creators (performing artists and songwriters)
3. A fair portion for distribution
4. A fair portion to other services such as A&R development support and marketing, whether done through labels or special services hired by the artists/creators.

Consider first #1 and 2, revenue in to the distributor, and then passing through to the artists (via whatever convoluted path through labels and rights organizations):

Sales of albums, and now album or track downloads (typically $1 or $10 for unlimited play), had been the mainstay of the business, but the flaw in their economics is clear, now that alternatives are more available.

- Buying music is a good value for the user only if they play it many times. Lightly played albums are very expensive per play. Conversely, heavily played albums are a huge bargain (one that neither the distributor not the artist fully shares in).
- The payment to the artists/creators (via whatever path) is roughly tied to unit sales, and so depends on how many people buy, not how much value they got (measured by how often they play it and other factors). That disproportionately favors production of pop hits over music with more subtle but perhaps more lasting appeal.

"All you can eat" (AYCE) subscriptions (typically $5 to 10 per month) to unlimited numbers of plays per month from a massive library (the "Celestial Jukebox") are gaining market share, but this too has perverse economics:

- Flat rate subscriptions have a one-size-fits-all price that actually fits very few. Ultimately the price must be set to earn the distributor a reasonable margin on average over a widely varying user base. Some will play many hours per day, resulting in little revenue pass through per track—or a net loss if the distributor pays rights holders a set fee per track. Others will be in a range that generates reasonable profit. Some will pay full price for light usage (for an excess profit), but many will refuse to pay the monthly fee at all, and stick with less profitable ad-supported free versions (or piracy). For light users, the standard monthly price will rightly seem exorbitant. *The irony here is that distributors earn little (or even lose money) on the dedicated music fans who should be their best customers!*
- Depending on the subscription service, the payment to the artists/creators (via whatever path) may be based on revenue, or on tracks played. If on revenue, the usage-related

inefficiency passes directly to the artists/creators. If on tracks, the artist/creator is less harmed by heavy users, but still loses out on those who opt out, or makes less on "free" versions with ads. Overall, this results in a licensing structure in which per track fees to rights holders must be very low because of this economic inefficiency. They may get paid per track, but as they say, the payments are woefully small—*not because the distributors are exploiting them, but because the distributors are caught in the middle of an inefficient pricing model.*

Neither of these current pricing models produce an economically sound result in which users pay at a level that corresponds to the value they receive. Prices are too high for many listeners, leading them to avoid paying at all. From an economic perspective, it would be far more efficient and fair to all if users paid based on usage (with some volume discount). But usage-dependent pricing models have generally been unpopular because users fear unpredictable billing levels and nasty surprises.

A Better Value Proposition with FairPay

FairPay promises to change the game—primarily, by making the total revenue pie bigger (by attracting more paying customers)—and secondarily, by making the artists/creators share of that pie bigger as well (by getting customers to pay based, in part, on the share going to the artists/creators). The essence is that it *enables prices to be individually set to match the value exchanged.* Instead of a flat price for (a) an unlimited number of plays of a purchased track or album *forever*, or (b) for an unlimited number of plays of any music in the catalog *per month*, FairPay can track to the amount of music played in any month, and can also factor in other aspects of value, including very subjective factors. (FairPay can also make song and album download models more effective, an item-oriented use, as explained earlier, but here we emphasize increasingly popular subscription models.)

With FairPay, users are given usage reports and suggested prices for their monthly listening, and get to decide what they think is fair—and give their reasons why. Distributors let them continue to do that as long as they generally pay an amount that seems fair enough to the distributor, given their individual context. Thus a light user might, in fairness, pay less than the $5 to 10 per month now charged, and a heavy user might be convinced that it is only fair that he should pay $15 or even more per month. (This process can be simplified once a pattern is developed, so that a customized pricing pattern can continue automatically, with the user intervening to change it only when desired.)

This expands the total revenue pie by exploiting the Long Tail of Customers. It gets some (existing, tall head) subscribers to pay more for their music, as heavy listeners, and as patrons of the music they love. It also brings in many more paying subscribers (the long tail, who now seek free alternatives like YouTube or other unlicensed sources because the subscription prices are too high)—even if many of those added subscribers pay less than the current set subscription price.

This usage sensitivity alone can help the artists/creators, since they can now get paid for more plays—and by more people. But FairPay can go farther, since it engages patrons in "dialogs about value" that center on the fairness of the price, and that fairness includes factors like how much of the price goes to the artists/creators. Daniel Ek of Spotify speaks of the need to increase transparency in this obscure area (as does the Copyright Office [McKinney 2015]), and FairPay can greatly leverage the power of that.

- Distributors (or their artists) can disclose their rates for passing through revenue to rights holders, so that customers can choose to use services that most generously sustain the artists/creators who produce the music—and can feel better about paying when they know a fair share is going to the artist/creator.
- FairPay can go further by enabling bonus payments to favorite artists, either by explicit direction of the user, or by indirect signals of value such as "thumbs up," inclusions in playlists, or frequency of play. Such adjustments might come out of the base pricing, or out of added patron bonus payments and might pass through 100 percent to rights holders.

All this can enable a more direct linkage between fans and artists, and a more direct exchange of value in which fans more fully take on the role of "patrons"—to sustain the artists who produce the music they care about. Crowdfunding models, such as PledgeMusic and Kickstarter, have demonstrated that serious fans are willing to spend much more than just the price of albums to support artists they care about. Amanda Palmer said:

> I see everybody arguing about what the value of music should be instead of what I think the bigger conversation is, which is that music has value, it's subjective and we're moving to a new era where the audience is taking more responsibility for supporting artists at whatever level. (Peoples 2013)

The core of FairPay is its systematic process for building individualized relationships in which creators/suppliers are rewarded by patrons for providing value that meets their individual needs. This can work through multiple levels of the value chain, to enable artists to most effectively tune and position their work to appeal to the audience who values and patronizes them.

FairPay creates a dynamically adaptive cycle of offers, prices, feedback, and further offers that rewards those who pay fairly and cuts off those who do not. Of course, this may not be very effective for a single music group (or game developer) who can make only infrequent offers of new products—but can be very effective for a music label or distributor that has a large and expanding library of products to offer for sale.

When it becomes clear that most of the price goes to the artist (and the people they chose to help them produce and distribute the music), and not just into the coffers of some faceless corporation, listeners will be more willing to pay a fair price for their music. FairPay can provide a process for working with each patron to jointly find that fair price.

Changing a Complex Industry

Making it happen will take work, and experimentation—and the entrenched powers of the music labels and the licensing rules and rights organizations will adapt slowly—but there is no reason why this can't be made to work far better than our current inefficient models.

FairPay may start most easily with the indies (independent artists/developers/studios/distributors), with their simpler business model infrastructure, and then migrate to the major labels (to the extent they remain relevant). Indies tend to be most hungry for exposure and growth of a fan base—and are the ones most willing to try PWYW—and thus have proven to be amenable to the risks of giving customers a say in pricing. (See discussion of indies and platforms in the following chapters.)

FairPay should be especially attractive for distributors who make it known that the artists (or game developers) get the dominant share of the revenue. Buyers will be more motivated to pay at reasonable levels if they know that their payments are going to the artist or developer—rewarding them for a good product, and providing the compensation they need to enable them to continue to produce future products. This can work for studios as well, especially if they position themselves as being very supportive of their artists (or even owned by them, as in the early days of United Artists).

Of course FairPay is also applicable to large recording studios and music and game distributors. As an item-oriented example, iTunes or Amazon could easily make FairPay offers across their entire inventory of downloadable music, or just across some subset. They might experiment with some selection of songs or albums. Perhaps they might start with less popular and familiar items (or whole genres) that might especially benefit from the try-before-you-set-the-price features of FairPay, to increase sales (and revenue) even if the average unit prices are reduced. Similarly, subscription services such as Spotify, Pandora, and Rhapsody could apply FairPay to their subscription offers (in much the same was as described for newspapers or video services in the previous chapter).

In summary, FairPay can be a win–win solution for all of the parties:

- *Growing the pie*—consumers will feel more respected and empowered by the added transparency, trust, and flexibility, and thus more willing to pay their fair share to support the music (or games) that they love.
  - o Some existing subscribers (such as light users) will pay less than the standard going rate, but the most dedicated fans will pay more.
  - o Most importantly, many of the large numbers who now decline to pay for conventional subscriptions (or downloads) as too costly (whether because of low usage or low

ability to pay) would be willing to pay something more reasonable, and still profitable, for a FairPay service—bringing
in a potentially large source of added revenue.

- *Sharing the pie*: This pie can then be divided more fairly
among the creators and value-adding intermediaries, based on
the detailed data on what the customers value and are willing
to reward.

Recorded music has huge value, and that value is consumed more
widely than ever. But our business models for capturing that value in the
form of consumer revenue, and distributing it fairly to the providers, are
broken so badly that musicians have turned to live concerts, merchandise,
and other revenue streams as the only way to survive (and some even
withhold their music from subscription services that they deem to pay
too poorly). FairPay promises to help reverse that economic failure. *With
a more direct linkage between value creation and monetary reward, the artist
can again find sustainable income from recorded music that is costly to create,
even if it can be distributed at almost no cost.*

CHAPTER 10

More Variations: App Stores, Indies, E-Books, Virality

The following sections survey a range of other industries, but assume a basic understanding of how FairPay works. As foundation, it is suggested that the previous chapters in this section, on FairPay in general and on the two in-depth examples of journalism and music be reviewed as well, recognizing that most of the points made there apply similarly to other industries. (More details and references at FPZLink.)

App Stores—A Distribution Platform Business, Item-Oriented, with Independent Creators and Distribution Intermediaries

FairPay adapts in interesting ways to industries where content/services are produced by independent creators but distributed to consumers through intermediaries, as seen in the example of the music business. This raises issues of passing costs and revenues through the value/supply chain, and how fairness can be managed across that. Such structures add both challenges and opportunities. FairPay promises to be quite effective in such industries, but where such relationships are complex and subject to industry inertia, a question is whether change will come from current industry participants or from disruptive new entrants.

App stores are a good example of where now-current distributors might have the power to apply FairPay without much disruption, given the large number of small independent product suppliers they could apply it to productively, and the simple revenue share models typically applied (typically a flat 10 to 30 percent). App stores now apply to a wide range of item types, not just software apps, but music, books, video/TV, and games. Of course app stores were themselves a recent disruption, but now they are very well positioned to step up to FairPay as a platform service.

Similar uses of FairPay apply in many industries that have a mix of independent creators and distributors/aggregators who work with them. Some, like music, are dominated by studios that manage creators, and some, like journalism mostly rely on internal creation. Some typical patterns:

- Journalism: Independent creation is generally not the case for major players—but there may be a new tier of distributors added above them, such as Blendle and Facebook.
- Music: As outlined, the studios (record labels) cooperate with distributors and represent the artists/creators, except for "indies" so this can get relatively complex.
- TV/video: A mix of models with growing presence of independent creators and distributors.
- E-Books: A mix of models with growing presence of independent creators (and some distributors).
- Games: Many independents, but some large studios.
- Software/apps: Many independents but large creators as well.

Software apps are especially interesting because of the diversity of players, the lack of pricing standards, and the severe pricing quandaries that result. Apps are becoming a huge business, but the vast majority of them are free. One analysis (Elmer-DeWitt 2010) suggests that 81 percent of iPhone app downloads *by volume* are free, even though other reports (Carvell 2010) indicate that only about 28 percent are free *by title*. This effect has been described as the "penny-gap"—the fact that products can "sell" like hotcakes when the price is zero, but demand drops precipitously when the price increases to just 1 cent. This makes price setting a major dilemma for app developers. (One very early attempt to solve this software pricing dilemma was "shareware," in which buyers could pay-*if*-you-want, at a suggested price—but that has been applied with little sophistication and proven only marginally successful.)

FairPay provides a way to bridge this penny gap—using its controlled form of *fair* pay what you want to still limit buyer risk, while strongly encouraging fair prices to sellers. As we know, FairPay works best within an ongoing buyer–seller relationship, so for an app store, it would be best implemented by the store operator (Apple or Google, or whoever) as a platform service. That way the feedback is collected across all purchases by a given customer, and can be applied to manage all future FairPay offers at the store. (More on platforms and shared reputation databases in Chapter 13.)

A FairPay process for an app store can be quite simple, much as described for item sales in Chapter 7. The store would implement and manage this process as a platform service, enabling developers (or providers of other content item types) to opt in, to offer their apps/items on FairPay terms, typically in tandem with the alternative of conventional pre-set prices. The result is that FairPay can be a win–win solution for the developers, the store, and the customers:

- Buyers will feel more respected and empowered by the added trust and flexibility. Some will pay less than the standard going rate, but some will pay more. Many who might not make a conventional paid purchase (because of the penny gap) might be willing to pay something reasonable for a Fair-Pay purchase, after they can see that they have gotten a useful app—the penny gap is smoothed over, and the developer and store get more revenue.

- Developers might set suggested target prices and other evaluation parameters, and could change those parameters or opt-out, depending on results. This could be structured to give the respective developers more or less visibility into the process, including the customization of suggested prices and the evaluations of fairness and gating of further FairPay offers applicable to their items.

- Developers need not feel that they must make their apps free in order to attract customers (since FairPay lets customers try-before-they-set-the-price, and if value is low, the price can be low—or zero). Developers willing to risk low prices to reach a large market could set liberal policies for fairness gating of their offers, while those who are more confident and demanding of generous pricing could set more restrictive policies. In this way new developers could target their offers based on customer reputation history derived from customer fairness history for other apps. Such history data and policies could be partitioned to be sensitive to different product categories, to address fairness behaviors that may vary depending on the category.

- The store can (with inputs from the developers) individually and dynamically tune the details of the offers and the process to encourage good payment levels, and to send free-riders back into the hard "paywall" of the conventional pre-set price.

App pricing has gotten even more complex because of current inefficiencies. As a form of freemium, many apps are now "free to download" (to maximize trial use), but require "in-app purchases" of premium features or upgrades to provide more than limited functionality. FairPay provides a much more flexible and efficient solution.

How Indies Can Lead a New Disruption

Given that FairPay is especially tuned to seeking fair payments to deserving sellers, some of the best early opportunities may be in businesses where this is a strong factor. This is especially relevant to independent content creators—and distributors who cater to them.

Music, games, and other content have been dominated by huge players—the Apple iTunes Store, which disrupted the old distribution models, and similarly by Google, and Amazon, which extended that to e-books. But there are many chinks in their armor—one is the shift to subscription models, such as music, where Pandora and Spotify have left Apple in catch-up mode. Another is that significant numbers of independent bands and game developers—and their fans—chafe at the economic constraints of the iTunes Store, and seek better ways to manage the value-exchange with their fans.

- As noted earlier, many indie artists and programmers have found PWYW pricing to be a surprisingly effective way to price, whether in temporary promotions such as Radiohead's, or as an ongoing model. Louis C. K. has offered a comedy video on PWYW for an extended period.

- Indie music distributors such as Bandcamp and Nogeno offer creators a range of payment models, including conventional fixed price and PWYW (with or without a minimum floor price).
- Bandcamp reported on their home page that "On name-your-price [PWYW] albums, fans pay an average of 50% more than whatever you set as your minimum." They offer guidance on using PWYW ... and on drawing on the customer appeal of the larger share they give to the artist.
- Others such as PledgeMusic have demonstrated significant revenue from crowdfunding, and strong ability to increase share of wallet by offering premium adjuncts.

As we know, FairPay adds a structured feedback process over an ongoing relationship, to make its "*Fair* Pay What You Want" model work better and more broadly. With regard to the indie opportunity there are two points to emphasize:

1. FairPay is especially relevant to indie distributors, because their music (or games) are mostly Long Tail content (not mass-market), where PWYW and FairPay can be especially effective in increasing revenue, and where sellers are willing to take more risk to get wide exposure. The artists are struggling for recognition (and compensation), and fans feel stronger connection to these struggling artists, and want to compensate them for their creations.

2. FairPay enables the aggregator/seller to establish an entirely new service role, as keeper of the FairPay reputation database that tracks how each of their individual customers behaves in terms of pricing fairness. That database provides important data usable by any potential seller (much like a credit rating database) to determine whether a customer pays fairly and should be entitled to make purchases on a FairPay basis (depending on the risk level implied by their reputation from previous purchases). The more complete the reputation database, the more effectively FairPay pricing works to maximize revenue and minimize risk.

This second point offers distribution aggregators such as Bandcamp and Nogeno a way to create a strategic asset that will differentiate them from competitors and raise a barrier to competition. Once FairPay gets critical mass, this database will have extensive pricing reputation data on many customers—something that will take time and money for a competitor to duplicate.

The combination of both points offers a path to disrupting the dominance of the iTunes Store (and Google and Amazon and other mass-market aggregators).

1. The Long Tail content focus of the indie market will be especially supportive of the FairPay model, because of the greater willingness of sellers to take a risk on their customers.

2. The customers will be disposed to behave well because they will know they are supporting the creators of the product (artists and/or programmers)—not the Apple 30 percent vig, or "the suits" in the studios.

3. The initial success will grow a FairPay reputation database that will increase the effectiveness of FairPay pricing and enable it to be used with decreasing risk for increasing numbers of products and customers.

4. That can greatly increase the appeal of the indie distributor, and widen its appeal to increasingly take share from iTunes and other mainstream aggregators.

Of course iTunes can offer FairPay as well, and build its own database. The indies would still have the advantage of a higher share going to the artist, and thus a better value proposition than the big guys. They might not take over the world, but they could disrupt the current models in a way that makes a better value proposition to consumers and creators, and increases the net opportunity for indies.

Creators Direct-to-Consumers—Extreme Disintermediation

Taking the deserving seller to fan connection to the extreme of full disintermediation might be a very interesting place to apply FairPay. Consider innovative possibilities for Creators Direct-to-Consumers (D2C), often referred to as Direct-to-Fan (D2F). We mentioned Radiohead, but other big name creators have made pioneering moves in the D2C direction, such as Amanda Palmer in music, Seth Godin in books, and Louis C. K. in comedy video. Here is how people like them can make much more money.

- They obviously know that by ditching the middleman and going straight to their public, they get a much larger piece of what they sell. And they clearly know how to reach their public without the help of a middleman, and that they and their public are partners in co-creation.
- They also know that PWYW can be a very effective way to reach their market, getting far more people to buy, and many of them to pay reasonably well. But they know that many pay poorly—PWYW is participative, but has only weak motivations for fairness.

FairPay offers them a new path to profit. It may not work well for a tiny catalog, like a few albums or books, but can be powerful for a prolific creator who can sustain an ongoing series of sales. For example:

- Individual songs from a growing collection of albums, offered in series, one at a time, or in small bundles ...
- Individual items from a growing catalog of book chapters, articles, podcasts, or videos ... (A 21st Century Charles Dickens?)

FairPay promises to produce far more sales than any set-price offer, and far more revenue and profit than any conventional PWYW offer. Any content producer who is prolific and well-known enough to draw an audience to a large or actively growing library of content could try FairPay on their own.

Of course scale is a factor for FairPay, which can be more effective when aggregating a larger collection of content that will sustain a more extended relationship with customers, and thus enable a better grounded feedback/control process. This might be done by teaming up with other content creators who appeal to the same customers, perhaps in a cooperative selling service. That brings us back to indie platform support services. There are opportunities all along this spectrum from individual creator D2C, to indie aggregators, to mainstream aggregators.

"E-Books Are Reading You"—How That Enables a New and Better Economics

"As New Services Track Habits, the E-Books Are Reading You" (Streitfeld 2013). While some view publishers tracking one's reading as creepy, it offers powerful benefits that are yet to fully emerge. Wouldn't it be good to pay for books depending on how you read them? This recent *New York Times* article highlights the instrumentation behind e-books and other digital media (long common for Web pages), and how distributors, publishers, and authors can use it to better understand their markets. People are talking about how Big Data enables "The Quantified Self"—think of this as "Quantified Media."

With FairPay, this gains greater value—and clear benefit to the reader. How much you have to pay for a book can depend on how you read it—how much, how long, how deeply, how repetitively. That data is indicative of the value you receive from the book. Why should what you pay to read it not depend on how you read it?

- Start a chapter or two and quit, and pay nothing—just like a Kindle free sample.
- Skim the whole book in 15 minutes and pay little or nothing—much like Amazon's "Look Inside."
- Read a novel all the way through and pay a normal price.
- Read it three times and pay a bit extra. Study a "how-to" book, highlight sections, and go back regularly over many months, and pay accordingly (but with a volume discount).
- Use six travel guides on four countries during a one-week cruise and pay the equivalent of buying one travel guide (see the next section).

Already, individual reader usage data is affecting pricing between distributors and publishers (as the *Times* article notes for book subscription offerings):

On Oyster, once a person reads more than 10 percent of the book, it is officially considered "read." Oyster then has to pay the publisher a standard wholesale fee. With Scribd, it is more complicated. If the reader reads more than 10 percent but less than 50 percent, it counts for a tenth of a sale. Above 50 percent, it is a full sale.

Offering a subscription service "introduces a sort of interesting business opportunity to collaborate with publishers rather than be at odds with them." What a thought! Sounds like a step toward win–win pricing models!

With FairPay, a similar win–win collaboration involves the reader as well. FairPay lets readers pay whatever they think is fair for books, based on how they read them. If the distributor agrees that is fair (factoring in any explanations offered) their subscription or buying privileges are continued. This removes the barrier of price from reading a book. It invites anyone with an interest to try a book, and only pay to the extent that they feel they got value from it. It allows those on limited budgets to apply discounts, and business readers to be expected to pay more, having derived greater value. It also strengthens the bond between the reader and author, where readers feel an obligation to pay to authors who give them a valuable reading experience (especially if they know a fair share really goes to the author). It also strengthens the bond between the reader and a publisher/distributor who curates access to the kind of e-books they value, and supports authors they value.

The Economics of Abundance—Post-Bundling— A Travel Guide Example

Abundance is a fundamental feature of the Internet. Content providers keep trying to wall-off their content (the artificial scarcity of "walled gardens"), but the manifest destiny of the Internet keeps breaking those walls down. Why can't we access anything we think we will value, and then pay a fair price for whatever that turned out to be? FairPay is a pricing model for the Internet age, the age of the infinite "Celestial Jukebox." That jukebox can extend far beyond music. Here we look at an example for books.

Travel guides on smartphones and tablets present a nice example of some of the richly flexible kinds of pricing behaviors that become feasible with FairPay. FairPay can enable nearly unlimited access to content from varied sources, while giving the providers of that content reasonable compensation for the value they provide. The following example suggests the sophistication that advanced uses of FairPay can provide. (More at FPZLink.)

A challenge in pricing travel guides (where pricing has not evolved much from the printed book mentality) is that different readers get very different levels of value, so set prices may be too high for some potential users and too low for others. What if I could have access to many guides, and pay based on the use I made of them? It is impractical to pre-set prices on such a flexible basis, but not so hard to do so after the fact (especially on FairPay's intuitive basis, aided with usage data).

Consider the range of situations for using a guide. On a small-ship cruise, I might stay a few days in two terminus cities, plus have day stops in half a dozen small towns in as many as five or six countries along the way (some with guided tours, some on my own). On that cruise I might want limited use of one or two guides for each of the countries visited, even though some small ports might have little or no coverage. (Similar variations might apply to heavy use of a guide on a first visit to a major city, and to light use on a later return visit, or to use of two complementary guides, one heavily, and one lightly.)

Paying a set price for each guide as usually packaged is not efficient. Buying even a single set of guides to all cities/countries visited on my cruise is a poor value proposition (likely well over $100), so I might not buy any. But I would happily pay a reasonable amount for light use of many guides. *Conventional pricing is lose–lose.*

Obviously it would be difficult for a publisher (or even a full-service bookseller such as Amazon or B&N) to set multifactor prices that worked for such extremes of usage. The beauty of FairPay is that they don't have to—I would set the price. Knowing the list price of guidebooks, I might feel that I am willing to spend $20 to $40 per week, if I am using my guide(s) heavily, and less if not. If I used multiple guides, I would want to divide my payment based on which I used most and which were most valuable (such as tipping me off to hidden "finds").

How can this work? I would not mind if the sellers had meters that recorded my usage ("reading me"), but I would be put off by knowing that there are set charges per page or minute of viewing, with a meter going ka-ching. I would be OK with such metrics of usage as *suggestive* of what I should pay, but not as a relentlessly ticking meter of unit charges (the old micropayment problem). With FairPay, I could have it my way.

Amazon (or Apple or whoever) could administer the store, collect the metered usage data, and let me set prices as I see fit. As long as I priced at reasonable levels (considering my usage), they would continue to let me get more guides (for my next trips) on a FairPay basis. If I did not pay well, they would cut me off and it would be back to the old way. For a return trip, they might offer use of an updated guide, and expect only modest added payment, resulting in another win for both me and the sellers.

Good for me, and the publisher(s). I could use guides at various cities on the cruise, and pay for the moderate level of usage that I would forego with conventional pricing. I would feel much better about being able to use and pay for guides accessed my way, not the way the publisher pre-packages them into "titles" that don't fit me—and so would be willing to pay at higher levels. The publisher and the store would get more from me, and I would be much happier about the fairness of the value exchange. This would also be most efficiently win–win if it worked across multiple publishers, to allow me to create mixed bundles.

Such FairPay offers might be structured as packages for specific trips, with pricing set by the user soon after the trip. Frequent travelers would place high value on the flexibility this offers, and be careful to pay at good rates to retain the privilege of doing the same for future trips. Occasional travelers, and those on tight budgets might pay at lower rates, but without FairPay, they might otherwise not buy guides at all. (To prevent low-paying customers from hopping from seller to seller to escape a bad reputation, the sellers might share their reputation data, just as with credit rating data.)

The bottom line: nearly ideal Internet economics. I get access to all the guides I feel I have use for (exploiting their near-zero marginal cost), and pay based on how I use them (based mostly on my intuitive allocation of value, grounded in the reality of usage data and publisher suggestions).

The publisher can sell to anyone who has use for the product, and get revenue commensurate with that use.

What I propose here is actually a form of "post-bundling." Another example is presented in Chapter 18 for cable TV channel bundles. Travel guide books are bundles of city guides, pre-packaged as a book. With e-books, and with cable TV, customers can build their own ad-hoc bundles on demand, and have them priced after the fact—pricing whatever bundle we assembled on a discounted basis comparable to the rates for set bundles. Why should custom bundles not be priced just as favorably?

Virality and Superdistribution

The viral nature of "the global village" has been recognized since the days of Marshall McLuhan, and social media is now a major factor in marketing, especially for content.

"Superdistribution" emerged in the 1980s and 1990s as a technology for generating revenue from viral distribution, but has yet to catch on broadly (Cox 1996). However, it has resurfaced with some success more recently, and suggests an interesting use-case for showing how FairPay readily adapts to a viral marketing context. BitTorrent introduced "gated" bundles, a new "relationship based" content superdistribution architecture in 2013 (Ha 2013). That is very aligned with the relationship-oriented monetization strategies of FairPay. Both exploit-free and "gated" offers, and both go beyond freemium by doing it in a way that relies deeply on partnerships with artists and other creators/producers of content. Gated Torrent Bundles and FairPay are both great ideas, and the combination promises to be even better.

Torrent Bundles provide a viral superdistribution technology designed to work with various forms of gating of content that is to be paid for, in a way designed to build a relationship. They provide a viral download that combines a portion of free content with a portion of "gated" content that can be unlocked in various ways, by linking to a gateway to premium content. These gated bundles are said to support pay gates, PWYW gates, or links to outside sites such as Netflix or iTunes.

That can be made even more flexible, by adding the option to open the gate on a gentler FairPay basis. A viral superdistribution context is one of the ways FairPay was designed to work. Anyone can redistribute bundles that contain FairPay offers, and the recipients can begin to establish their own FairPay relationships (and reputations) to get the added content (if not already in a FairPay relationship). Of course criteria for pricing of content received virally would be expected to be relatively lenient, to encourage risk-free sampling, so that both senders and recipients feel well treated. (More at FPZLink.)

Both viral superdistribution and micropayments are appealing strategies that are seemingly well-suited to the Internet, but they have failed to achieve market success with regard to monetization. The softer handling of pricing in a relationship that FairPay enables could be the missing link that eliminates the major hurdle to getting both consumers and businesses to embrace these techniques.

CHAPTER 11

FairPay for Non-Digital Services

While digital services have the nearly free replication that is particularly well leveraged by FairPay, there are interesting prospects more widely. This chapter considers a few representative examples, including some where replication costs are high. As we will see, such costs may not be too much of an impediment if the sales are promotional or perishable, or if a price floor that covers marginal costs can be applied.

A FairPay Coupon/Trials Service—A Better Groupon

Trial coupons (from aggregators such as Groupon) can be a very effective way to attract new customers, but as generally done, this process tends to attract bargain-hunters—who may not be the customers a business really wants to attract. FairPay promises to enable a better way to attract your real target market.

FairPay has significant potential for use with real products and services, especially for experience goods, where the true value is only apparent after having the experience. A Groupon-like service could offer "coupons" for trial offers, such as for restaurants, service establishments, and the like, much as now, but based on FairPay pricing. While this would be hard for a single promotional seller to do, a promotional platform such as Groupon can build continuing relationships with individual customers to optimize offers for a continuing stream of merchants.

For example, for the case of a restaurant (which has significant marginal costs), the offers may be framed so that the customer is told they can pay any price they want, but if not at least a suggested percentage (maybe 50 percent, maybe more), they must explain why they think that is fair (with a few multiple choice questions that are easily scored automatically).

- They might also be told that a suggested fair price should
  be between 25 percent and 75 percent of the normal billed
  price. This reflects the win–win objective of providing a
  discount for taking the risk of a disappointing meal, but
  with the idea that even a disappointing meal is usually worth
  something (say 25 percent of full price), and a very good
  meal deserves a good price, even as a trial (say 75 percent
  of full price).
- The customer might be free to pay zero, but only in truly rare
  cases would that not be taken as a black mark on their reputation score that might exclude them from most or all future
  offers (exceptions would be for customers who have built a
  reputation for paying fairly).
- This pricing could be set directly with the aggregator right
  after the meal (such as in a mobile app), who would then
  settle with the restaurant privately.

By doing this over a series of offers, the aggregator can character-
ize each customer with a FairPay reputation, maintain that in a database
(along with rich, transaction-level detail on what they pay well for and
what they do not—and why), and use that reputation data to target additional offers.

- Those merchants most eager to attract customers will make
  offers to a wide range of prospects (with correspondingly
  high risk).
- More established or selective merchants might limit offers
  to those who have already gained a reputation for paying
  fairly (thus taking relatively low risk, from more valuable
  customers).
- The aggregator can also limit the number of offers that a particular merchant makes to untested customers with unknown
  fairness reputation, to limit the risk even for marginal
  merchants.

The benefit to customers is that those who are willing to pay fairly when
they get value can be given trial offers for quality establishments that they

might be likely to revisit. It can be made clear that customers who price at above the suggested value can generally expect to become eligible for more attractive offers, and those who price below that value will generally get less desirable offers. Some customers will price for quality and style, and some will price for the biggest discounts they can get (as long as they do not squeeze too hard). But offer flow will vary accordingly.

The benefit to merchants is that they can target the prospects most likely to appreciate what they offer, in a way that calibrates their risk. Some will seek many new customers at relatively high risk, while others will be selective, and take minimal risk. Thus even high-quality restaurants might use this to expand their market selectively and efficiently, not only the less distinguished restaurants that seem to be typical of Groupon (a vicious cycle race to the bottom).

The benefit to the aggregator is not only a more effective coupon business, and a new broader range of customers and merchants participating, but a valuable new database of very fine-grained data on customer value perceptions and willingness to pay. Again, this FairPay reputation database can become a very valuable asset in itself. (And the aggregator can maintain the privacy of the customer data by not revealing the data to the merchants, but just using it internally to manage the offer process based on merchant-specified criteria, much as many ad-targeting services do.) (See Chapter 13.)

This can also apply to services analogous to Priceline's, especially for products such as hotel rooms that have a high experience good aspect. A number of hotels already do pay-what-you-want (PWYW) offers at off times, so FairPay is a clearly attractive alternative. (Note that the "Name Your Price" feature of Priceline is very different from PWYW, and from the Fair PWYW approach of FairPay, since with Priceline the seller can and will reject your price if it is lower than his secret minimum price. With FairPay your price is never rejected—you just won't be allowed to continue setting unfairly low prices more than very rarely.)

The experience of many restaurants, theaters, hotels, and other businesses who have tried PWYW offers serve as a proven reference point in the non-digital world. Even without the reputation tracking controls that FairPay applies to limit free-riding, PWYW has proven effective in many such situations, including the long running example of the Panera Cares restaurant chain. (More in Chapter 20, and FPZLink.)

FairPay for Costly Real Products

The coupon service just described is promotional, but can FairPay work on a more routine basis for real products that have significant replication cost? Consider a fashion retailer like Everlane or an artisan marketplace like Etsy? There are actually some very interesting opportunities.

The trick is very simple: *set a minimum price floor* that allows the buyer to set whatever price they want *above that minimum*. This can ensure that sales are not at a loss, and limit the FairPay adaptation process to apply only to the additional value share that the seller should receive above their cost. This builds on the simpler idea of PWYW with a price floor, which has been common. (Of course value does not always exceed the producer's cost, so even the minimum can sometimes be an issue.)

A nice example of conventional PWYW with a floor was provided by fashion e-tailer Everlane.com. In 2015 they had a five-day Christmas sale that offered an array of items at any of three different prices. For example, a woman's coat said to normally sell for $250 was offered for any of three prices, and a mouseover popup frames the rationale for each of those options:

- "$110: $0 to Everlane. This only covers our cost of production and shipping."
- "$132: $22 extra to Everlane. This helps to cover production, shipping, and overhead for our 70-person team."
- "$225: $115 extra for Everlane. This helps cover production shipping, our team, and allows us to invest in growth. Thanks!"

FairPay would enable such sales to become a regular option for selected customers (including those found to pay well on special sales like this Christmas sale). For customers who develop very good reputations for pricing fairness, many items might be offered that way all the time. For customers who gain moderately good fairness reputations, such offers might be more limited.

FairPay with a Price Floor–for Retailers and Marketplaces

Building on this example for a single retailer, consider how FairPay with a price floor can also apply to a platform for serving many sellers, like Etsy. com, a marketplace for many designers and artisans:

- The process would be explained up-front, so that buyers and sellers understand that the initial price is just a base price that only covers the cost of the product (and perhaps a very small profit margin), but that buyers who are happy with the product are expected to pay more than that, once they see the value of what they have gotten.
- The seller could post a suggested bonus price (with profit margin), but buyers could decide to price higher or lower, based on their own judgment of fair value.
  - *Buyer risk is much less than at full price.* Refund options could still be provided to deal with serious dissatisfaction over even the "at-cost" base price. However, with the lower base price, fewer buyers would be so unhappy that they would wish to bother with a return for refund. Many would be willing to keep a marginally satisfactory product at a "bargain" price, given that the value is now known, and there is no further effort to doing that.
  - *Seller risk is low*, because they will at least cover their costs (except for a smaller than usual number of returns for refund).
  - *Both benefit by getting more customers to try the product.*
  - *The bigger benefit is in cooperatively seeking a fair profit margin*. Buyers who are happy can decide just how happy they are, considering all relevant factors, now that the value is known—and can set the bonus prices accordingly. Sometimes this process might lead to a price below a conventional price, sometimes above, but in any case it leads to profitable repeat customers.

The reason this is important is the Long Tail of Customers. Some buyers (the tall head) will happily pay more than a conventionally pre-set price, and that generates added revenue. Many buyers (the long tail) will be unwilling to pay a conventionally pre-set price, but would be willing to buy the product at the lower base price, and then consider adding a bonus. Any added bonus is added profit. Thus the seller sells more products and makes more buyers happy.

- This can work especially well for quality producers who delight their customers and motivate them to pay generously by triggering the use of communal norms. If Everlane's experience is like that of other PWYW vendors, positioning as a dedicated provider of quality and service can elicit high levels of fairness under communal norms.
- In the case of artisanal/craft products like on Etsy—and building on the person-to-person nature of sales in such a marketplace—communal norms of fairness should be especially relevant to motivating high levels of generosity.

Why Would Price Floors Work?

Consider the lessons of conventional PWYW offers:

- PWYW has proven reasonably effective for both virtual and real products/services. People can be motivated to willingly pay fairly even when they do not have to.
- Many sellers of digital products such as music and games have done PWYW offers with a minimum price set to at least cover download and credit card transaction costs, with good results. (Additional evidence may come from sellers such as Everlane.)
- Research studies suggest that price floors can be effective, but there is a framing downside to work around—setting a minimum can signal a lack of trust in the buyer, or give the impression that a fair price is not much above the minimum.
- In the case of real goods with substantial costs, it seems likely that the risk-mitigation of a price floor is more important than the signaling concerns. Care in framing that the floor

price alone is not really fair—in that it provides no profit and is thus not sustainable—can help push generosity upward—as can care in how the suggested profit margin is framed.

So it seems there is good reason to think this could work well for many real goods. Everlane seems a promising example, as a retailer building an image for value, fairness, and transparency. Similar advantages are applicable for other design/craft/artisan products—the seller can emphasize the human value of the artisan. Such use of FairPay could benefit a multiseller marketplace like Etsy, especially where buyers are unsure what to expect from a seller they do not know (and vice versa). This could be good for the buyer, good for the seller, and good for the marketplace.

I have not seen any reports on Everlane's PWYW results, and when the initial press reports hit, some were skeptical. But it is clear that we are at very early stages of understanding how to do participatory pricing most effectively (and getting consumers to understand how to play the game). I believe Everlane is on the right track, and that with proper framing of the offer, and what is expected of the customer, PWYW—and more advanced variations on it, like FairPay—will change how we buy things.

One simple enhancement might improve Everlane's results, even without the full FairPay feedback/tracking process: Let people *pay the base price up-front*, and then follow up to ask them to *decide on the bonus price after they receive the product and know how they like it*. This would be only a bit more complex to do, would still assure that costs are covered, but would gain all the benefits of post-experience pricing. Instead of wondering if I will really like the coat, and pricing low, because I am afraid to end up disappointed, I would know how much I liked it, and not have had to discount from what I now see to be fair.

Could it work for very high-end products—such as for Tiffany? Perhaps not so well, since at the very high end, high set prices are a signal of exclusivity—a vendor with cachet like Tiffany can command prices that less prestigious brands cannot. For that reason, I would guess Tiffany will be among the last places to try FairPay for its very costly core products. But even Tiffany has extra perks and value-added services that might benefit from FairPay. And who knows what surprising variations might become workable once FairPay becomes widely used and understood?

CHAPTER 12

FairPay for Nonprofit Organizations

FairPay also promises to dramatically enhance fund-raising for nonprofits. What better sector to benefit from the *fairness* that FairPay elicits?

Consider the spectrum from more service oriented to more charity oriented:

- Cooperatives that operate much like a business, but with all profits shared by the members.
- Professional organizations that may offer publications, conferences, certifications, and other benefits.
- Cultural organizations such as museums that may offer exhibits, facilities, and events.
- Secular or religious organizations that may cover a wide spectrum of direct services such as food, housing, schools, hospitals, and museums, and have a wide mix of direct customer recipients and indirect customer benefactors.

"Customers" are central across this spectrum, but with variations in expectations of how pricing applies:

- *In traditional for-profit business exchange*, customers are generally expected to pay enough to sustain the enterprise. (But even here, there are social values, such as in the business of journalism, and more generally in various "social" and "environmental" bottom lines, and in "benefit corporations.")
- *In nonprofits* that deliver services for fees, direct customers are expected to pay for services, but often with the help of subsidies from benefactors (indirect customers) who give donations to make those services more affordable.

- *In pure charities*, direct customers may not be expected to pay at all, and benefactors are needed to donate enough to sustain that.

FairPay provides new and better way to address the complex issues of pricing and sustainability across this spectrum. Consider how this works for the two different (but often overlapping) kinds of customers:

- *Recipients*—direct customers of direct services (the mission). Here, pricing takes on two interrelated dimensions—what is the fair value of the service, and what is the fair contribution from the recipient (to both the cost of the service, and to the added overheads needed to sustain the organization).
- *Benefactors*—indirect customers of indirect services (the altruistic value of supporting services to others, and the value of being a benefactor, including perks and recognition). Here, the key dimensions are the value of services to others enabled by the benefactor's donations, and the value of indirect benefits to the benefactor.

The details will vary with the type of customer and the nature of the organization and mission, but *the essential task is the same—to generate sustaining revenue by setting prices that make the value proposition be "win–win."*

Of course these factors are difficult to quantify in any precise and objective way, but the beauty of FairPay is that it puts value into personal terms, with all the nuance of human evaluation. Value setting need not be precise, as long as it is done through flexible and open dialog.

- Organizations can frame the value they think they provide in terms of whatever metrics are available (and the metrics are becoming increasingly meaningful).
- Customers (direct or indirect) can respond by factoring in whatever aspects of value they think important, including their perceptions of what is reported to them, plus any positive or negative factors they think important, including ability and willingness to pay. Multiple choice options (with some interpretation of free-text comments) can enable this to be

automatically scored and factored into assessments of whether customer-set prices are fair.

- The organization can offer "carrots" to encourage generosity, and gently withhold privileges or perks when "sticks" are needed.

FairPay provides a dynamic, emergent process for both sides to learn how to make the relationship maximally win–win. That can bring the organization more customers (recipients and benefactors) and get more share of wallet (the amount that the customers can justify and afford to give).

CHAPTER 13

FairPay Reputation Management—Databases and Platforms

Fairness Reputation Data and the Scale Economies of Platforms

We have seen that FairPay applies to individual businesses and aggregators, and the central role of the FairPay reputation database to manage offers (FairPay credit), as well as providing a treasure trove of marketing data. The FairPay reputation database captures detailed data for each customer on how they set prices for what, in what contexts. This new kind of very fine-grained market data could become very valuable. This chapter examines both the power of the database, and the power of a platform service that serves multiple sellers or merchants. Each has significant power individually, but here we address them in combination to highlight these synergies.

Reputation management: To recap from other sections, here is how this database (the Cloud of Value) is central to making FairPay profitable and manageable. The seller (and/or platform) can track how individual buyers respond to individual offers (and sellers), to learn how fairly a buyer sets prices for what kinds of products (and from what kinds of sellers). This provides a database on value perceptions and fairness reputation for each buyer that can be used to manage what is offered to specific buyers (by which sellers), so that sellers can control their risk and nudge individual buyers to maximize their fairness.

- Offers can be restricted to only those buyers who have a reputation for pricing fairly for the class of product being offered, so that sellers have a reasonable expectation that they will set a fair price.

o *For known buyers*, sellers can decide how much risk they want to take and how wide a market reach they want. Those who prefer a lower number of sales at higher prices can limit their offers to those known to price generously. Those more eager to expand the quantity they sell, at some greater risk to their profit margin, can expose offers to a broader segment of buyers who price fairly but less generously.

o For *unknown* buyers, some sellers will set liberal fairness thresholds for some products, so that new customer behavior can be learned at manageable risk. They may do this with selected product lines (or for limited promotions like Everlane's Christmas sale) that they can use for testing. Tighter fairness thresholds can be applied for sellers or product categories for which they want only more generous buyers.

• This mechanism gives a buyer a strong incentive to price fairly and even generously, to maximize the number and quality of offers they see. Buyers will know that it is the most desirable offers (and the most desirable sellers in a multivendor marketplace) that set the tightest fairness thresholds—so the less generous they are, the fewer top quality offers they can expect to see in the future.

Platforms: Given the investment needed for the software to manage the customer journey with these dialogs about value, and the resulting reputation data, clearly there are Software as a Service (SaaS) opportunities (such as extensions of services from companies such as Zuora and Salesforce, or new offerings). There is an economy of scale just in the processing software, but *the power of a common platform is greatly expanded when combined with a shared FairPay reputation database.*

Databases: *FairPay data gains added power in the context of a cross-vendor reputation management platform:*

• FairPay reputations for individual buyers can be tracked and applied across sellers.

- Sellers can maintain control of offer terms and gating, but manage this better based on a shared FairPay reputation database that has much broader scope.
  - Sellers considering a new buyer (to them) can see if the buyer has already developed a good or bad FairPay reputation in relationships with other sellers, and can then design their offers accordingly.
  - Buyers know that their FairPay reputation is a valuable asset, that enables them to *get more and better offers from a diversity of merchants*, and that *compromising that reputation can have real consequences*, by limiting future offers—a wider scope makes this more important, just as with credit data.
- The FairPay reputation database becomes a strategic asset to the platform provider, attracting sellers, and creating a significant barrier to competitors. Again, much like a credit rating database.

Of course this FairPay reputation data is sensitive and personal, much like credit rating data. Care will have to be taken for its privacy protection and how it is used. Consumer privacy can be protected by opt-in provisions and other protections. There are many ways to limit what data individual sellers can see from other sellers (including the option of none at all other than a simple rating or go/no-go indicator). One measure that could be important to any platform service that offers use of such data to multiple vendors is to make access indirect:

- The data aggregator might not expose the fairness data, itself, to the independent merchants. Instead, the merchants could specify rules for the selective "gating" of offers, which specify that their offers are to be made only to customers who have a fairness reputation rating that exceeds some threshold.
- The marketplace can then simply avoid matching a buyer to offers from sellers who set a fairness reputation rating threshold that is higher than the buyer's fairness reputation rating. That way the seller might know only that positive responses

were from those who did exceed that threshold, without divulging any buyer's actual rating.

- Similarly the amount of FairPay credit outstanding (the estimated value of services provided and not yet priced and paid for) could be limited to merchant-specified levels, again without letting the merchant know the individual reputations.
- Thus, all the seller knows about the buyer is that any buyer who sees their offer has at least the desired fairness rating.

While this is data that could make consumers uncomfortable, if not managed responsibly, it also enables consumers to be granted significant new powers to set prices. Transparency facilitates win–win. Positioning FairPay as a privilege—one that offers significant pricing power in exchange for a responsibility for fairness—should make that a bargain worth taking—power in exchange for information.

There is also potential for both businesses and consumers to have shared access to portions of this data. Business could use it (perhaps anonymized) to show a customer how other customers set prices for comparable services as support for the fairness of a suggested price. And of course consumers might want access to information on how other consumers set prices, to ensure that their own fairness and generosity is more or less consistent with the behavior of others.

Note that complementary fairness information services for consumers might arise—providing data on the fairness of companies. This could include data both on how demanding or forgiving they are in how they rate their customers, and also on how customers rate the company's fairness—including relevant data on the specific factors and contexts involved. (More in Chapter 23.)

As we move beyond single-company reputation databases, it will take some time to shake down appropriate management policies for wider use, sharing, and disclosure of such data, but that seems just a matter of experimentation and learning. And conventional pricing (without fairness data) can always remain the fallback option for those customers who prefer not to engage in the level of dialog and transparency this invisible handshake entails.

Entrepreneur Alert!

Building a FairPay platform and database business could be an opportunity with huge leverage. There are a wide variety of ways to do this, as we have touched on. These could provide first-mover advantages that build network effects and create significant barriers to competitors. Moving toward increasingly specific functional focus, the openings to build a business that exploits FairPay and the new kinds of data it creates range from:

- *Basic content/product/service businesses*—just add FairPay as an attractive new relationship option to any such business.
- *Aggregated content/product/service businesses*—build or enhance a platform that serves multiple vendors or acts as a multisided marketplace hub.
- *Transactions as a Service (TaaS) platforms*—concentrate on the transaction back-end to some class of businesses, much like Zuora and Recurly do for subscriptions, and others do for item-oriented sales.
- *Pricing as a Service (PaaS) platforms*—concentrate on just the pricing and related FairPay fairness reputation and FairPay credit tracking and offer gating.

New Ecosystems of Value

This harks back to the Cloud of Value. We can expect whole new Ecosystems of Value to develop around this new kind of value data and the new support services it enables. We have surveyed a wide range of use-cases for FairPay (summarized in the short list just previously), but there are many more. Some of these may emerge quickly, others only after much foundation work is laid. A few suggestive examples follow.

Pricing as a Service platforms. This could be applied on a very broad horizontal basis. We have seen how FairPay ties pricing into a relationship tracking and management service that can pool merchant experience much like a credit rating service. This has obvious relevance to platform providers such as Amazon, Apple, and Google, but why not an even broader service from credit card companies such as American Express, MasterCard, Visa, or PayPal? Such companies could provide a platform for pricing, tracking, and FairPay credit management, as just another service to the huge numbers of merchants they serve. (As is common, such platforms could integrate with merchant systems via APIs—application program interfaces.)

Actor-to-Actor (A2A) hubs (or aggregators). We touched earlier on the potential for Creator-to-Consumer sales by artists, but clearly the same can apply to any kind of product or service, even Consumer-to-Consumer (C2C), so we should be thinking broadly of Actor-to-Actor hubs. These could include creators or producers of other products/services, and can include individuals or businesses on any of the sides, much like eBay, as well as the Etsy-like example, or any kind of multisided marketplace hub.

Large or small businesses. It is hard to predict just how FairPay and related strategies will develop. Large selling organizations and large platforms can apply very sophisticated methods to the FairPay feedback and process management controls, but smaller sellers who elicit a high feeling of deservedness can leverage that to their advantage, drawing on favorable communal norms, even with just rudimentary platform support. We have very interesting array of roads ahead. The next chapter considers how we can start small and then build.

CHAPTER 14

Learning the New Logic— Low-Risk Testing, Sweet Spots, and Continuous Adaptation

How to start? Find the sweet spots. Established businesses will want to do controlled testing in a restricted environment to learn how these methods work and tune the process before putting mainstream revenues at risk. Even start-ups will want to move in managed stages. This chapter explores some strategies for doing that, and growing from there.

Be sure to keep an open mind. The starting points proposed here need to be tested. The paths to increasing sophistication and variations in the next chapter should be kept in mind as well. Such enhancements might turn out to be important to achieving success early on.

Perhaps the most promising areas to consider for proof of concept testing in small, controlled trials—that do not put profit or reputation at much risk—are the following three:

- *Retention*—win-back offers to subscribers who are asking to cancel (but had previously seen value).
- *Acquisition*—offers to potential new customers in selected segments that might see new value.
- *Premium* "club" or "patron" tiers—offers to existing customers known to recognize the value.

Other possibilities include selection of test populations in any way that limits risk and targets segments that may appreciate the value of the offering and the personalized value proposition, such as:

- Usage or style segments
- Content segments (such as long-tail items, or by genre)
- Device segments
- Family plans
- Segments that can highlight "deserving" sellers
- Trials, specials, coupons
- Distinct branding or white label offers.

Find the Sweet Spots

A key factor is that FairPay involves behavior change by consumers. It is a shift back to behavior norms that are natural and were common through much of history, but still a change, and some customer segments will adapt more readily than others. Some will be slow to shift from zero-sum thinking, while others will jump at the opportunity. *The trick will be to find low-hanging fruit—lines of business with customer segments who are most disposed to welcome this new logic.*

- The best customers to start with will be those who are disposed to generosity. That may include "superfans" who are loyal and perceive high value, and loyal customers of providers who demonstrably deserve generosity for delivering high quality, service, and social value.
- The best prospects will also be disposed to strong cooperation—receptive customers who are thrilled to share pricing responsibility—and are willing to bear some modest burden to do that right.

That will serve as the thin end of the wedge of behavior change. The initial strategy should be to find these sweet spots and do low-risk controlled tests there. Businesses and customers will begin to see good results and learn how to apply this kind of adaptively win–win strategy. That will generate a viral effect to attract more customers to the game, and lead a growing range of firms to create FairPay zones. (Background on the behavioral economics of this is in Chapter 20.)

Retention: Winning Back Lost Customers Before They Get Lost

For existing subscription businesses, retention is so important and such an ideal place to do limited testing of FairPay that it may border on irresponsible not to seriously consider testing that. It is widely accepted that retention is the key to profitability.

- Keeping good customers is increasingly central to maximizing profit and customer lifetime value (CLV), as highlighted in the March 2016 HBR Idea Watch "Winning Back Lost Customers" (Greig 2016). Companies are realizing that customer acquisition is very costly, and saps profits if churn is high. Win-back offers must be personalized more smartly, to present the right value proposition to the right customer.
- Retention win-back offers are already made on a one-to-one basis to selected customers who are already well known to the business, and have a record of valuing the product. The problem is not their failure to recognize value, but a misalignment of perceived value with the set price—that is exactly the problem FairPay is designed to solve.
- Because win-back offers are often made one-to-one, typically using costly human agents, testing of FairPay can be limited, controlled, and done with varying levels of automation. This enables careful selection of test subjects, tight control of offer policies, and use of semiautomated, simple decision rules prior to investing in more complex automation.
- Win-back offers are naturally viewed by both parties as trials, so tests can be framed as limited-time special programs that can be ended at the business's discretion.

So, why not try enhancing win-back efforts:

1. Automatically create personalized win-back offers that are adaptively win–win.

2. Shift from reactively trying to win back customers who are almost lost—to proactively enhancing the customer journey to retain them before they get lost at all.

FairPay can initially be trialed as adding a new, more automated, and more efficiently win–win tool. But FairPay leads to a deeper break-through—to put proactive retention directly into every customer journey loyalty loop.

- We know that an ounce of prevention is worth a pound of cure, but any retention strategy is just a belated attempt to cure a customer's dissatisfaction with the value proposition after it has become a serious problem.
- When proactively integrated into the customer journey loyalty loop, FairPay creates ongoing dialogs about value, so that potentially good customers are routinely engaged to jointly craft personalized value propositions, long before they approach the point of being lost.
- Just as smart marketers are building loyalty loops into every cycle of the customer journey, they can do the same for value and retention.
- Think loyalty loop = retention loop.

Key retention tasks are selecting the right customers to try to retain (using propensity models), and finding the right value propositions to present successful win-back offers tailored to those individual customers. Key success parameters for a retention strategy are both cost and return on investment (ROI). Typical options include discounts, service upgrades, and combinations of the two, and results can be enhanced by tailoring the nature of the offer—and whether to make an offer—to the reasons a customer seeks to cancel. The HBR article gives the example of how Cox Communications is getting smarter about customizing its retention offers to individual customers of its cable TV and Internet services, and triggering such offers at the right points in their customer journeys. A big step in the right direction—of customizing the pricing and features of their offers—but still doing it in a costly manner, relying on human intervention, on a reactive exception basis.

Consider two stages of development: first at doing this better and more automatically, and then at doing it more widely and proactively.

Retention Level 1: Adaptively Customizing Retention Offers—Try More Effective Pricing for Those Who Are Demanding It

First consider how FairPay can enhance conventional win-back offers. *FairPay generates an ongoing multivariate pricing experiment with each customer.*

- FairPay can be offered to limited numbers of customers seeking to cancel, framed as a special trial offer that will be continued only if they price fairly, and only if enough other customers show that they, too, will set prices fairly.
- FairPay retention options can be offered selectively to known customers, based on data that suggests which ones are worth keeping and which ones seem most likely to demonstrate the positive social value orientation that will lead them to set prices fairly—using strategies along the lines outlined in the HBR article.
- Selection criteria might further isolate testing of FairPay to those customers with a history of relatively light usage—for which discounted prices would be fair—a strong incentive, and still very profitable.
- FairPay can be tested in controlled populations, and framed as a special experimental offer, to minimize risk—a privilege that will be continued only if enough customers cooperate, and revocable for any customer who is not reasonable.

It is essential to be smart about what offers to make to which customers. FairPay offers an automatically adaptive way to do that, with offers that are flexible and constantly tuned to individual customer value perceptions.

Customers seeking to cancel are sending the message that the conventional value proposition does not work for them. The way to retain them is to find a profitable value proposition that does work for their particular situation and point in time. FairPay offers an automatically adaptive process for doing just that.

This first stage effectively provides a low-risk test—to try more effective pricing, but only for those customers who are about to leave if they do not get something better. Subscription businesses face not only simple questions of price, but also the dilemma of whether to apply usage-based pricing (which consumers find unfriendly and subject to nasty surprises), or all-you-can-eat pricing (a one-size-fits-all price that is too high for light users and too low for heavy users). FairPay's adaptive pricing can work better than either option, adding its new kind of value focus to blend the best aspects of both plans in a dynamically adaptive way. Those customers who reject the conventional pricing are a natural place to try this new and more flexible alternative on a limited basis.

The beauty of FairPay retention offers is that they are self-adjusting. Once you learn how to set key business rules for what to offer, to whom, and when, it then takes a minimum of live intervention by costly and hard-to-manage support staff. Customized FairPay offers can be made automatically, quickly, and at low cost, to every customer worth keeping.

Based on what you learn in such a limited trial, you may find it desirable to expand it, refine it, and extend it more widely—to apply FairPay to customer acquisition, special premium/loyalty programs, and perhaps even to your core subscription pricing.

Retention Level 2: Proactive Retention—Seeking Win–Win All the Time

Managing retention on an exception basis is counterproductive. *Do you let your spouse feel neglected or abused and ignore that until they ask for a divorce?* If customizing value propositions makes sense when customers ask to cancel, wouldn't that be much more effective before they get so far gone? Why wait until then to begin dialog on the issues? Think about what listening to your customers really means. Real listening may seem impractical, but FairPay provides a process for doing that efficiently and profitably.

Why are we content with poor value propositions for those customers who don't take the trouble to complain? Why do we wait for them to cancel? It may seem nice to have quietly dissatisfied customers on auto-renew—and hope they will never think about what they are paying and what they are getting—but is that really the way to grow loyalty?

Maybe we would have more and better customers if we tried to proactively find better value propositions for all of them. That is what FairPay is designed to do. Once you have learned the basics of managing dynamically adaptive FairPay retention offers, why not extend that to all of your regular customers?—at least for all of those who seem to value your product, and who demonstrate their fairness during an initial learning period. (Those who do not prove to be fair can be returned to the conventional set-price plans.)

The whole point of FairPay is to continuously seek win–win relationships that customers are satisfied with. It gives early warning of dissatisfaction, and provides processes for resolving issues—as customers become aware of them, and long before they ask to cancel. The idea is to build consideration of value—and how that drives retention—directly into the loyalty loop, for every cycle of each customer journey.

Premium "Club"/"Patron" Segments and Loyalty Programs

Premium tiers and loyalty programs have particularly strong promise of good results with FairPay because they target your best, most engaged, and loyal customers. Tests can be framed as trials, and loyal customers can be enlisted much as for focus groups. The *New York Times* provides an excellent example, having introduced *Times Premier* in 2014 (without FairPay, at $10 per four weeks), at which time I did a blog post proposing FairPay as a better alternative.

"For those with a curiosity that matches our own," the *Times'* pitch read, but what I was most curious about is whether and how I would value it. ... And whether the value to me would be consistent, or highly variable and hard to predict. (Apparently *Times Premier* did not meet objectives and was reintroduced in 2015 as *Times Insider*. I did try *Times Premier*, and canceled after the four-week trial. I have since subscribed to *Insider*, and don't see much difference, but, as an ongoing experiment, have acquiesced to this unsatisfying value proposition.)

The *Times'* metered paywall has been working better than many feared, but is obviously leaving money on the table from loyal, engaged readers who can and would pay more for *Times'* journalism and extras. *Premier/*

Insider attempt to capture that value, but, like the old "Godfather"-inspired joke, *they have made me an offer I cannot understand.* As I said at the time:

- It offers me a combination of new features, some in specific quantities.
- I don't know what these are, have never seen many of them, have no idea if I will like them. And, even if I do like some of them, how many will I want in any given four-week cycle?
- Some sound interesting, and some not at all.
- Even after I have tried them, I expect my desire and opportunity to enjoy them will vary and might decrease over time.
- I may want more than the included number of some features, while having no interest in others.

I can afford the extra $10 per four weeks cost, but have no confidence that I will value the service.

- Maybe I might try it and, if not too disappointed, just continue to pay the $10 without much thought (as the *Times* might hope)—but profiting from my inattention leaves me feeling exploited.
- Alternatively I might try it for a while, then cancel—even if I would be willing to pay something for the occasional feature—leaving both me and the *Times* losers.
- In any case, I feel little temptation to even bother—again leaving both me and the *Times* losers.

The core problem is a rigid, one-size-fits-all pricing scheme—for a time- and quantity-varying experience good that is offered to diverse customers with different and time-varying needs.

I had previously suggested to the *Times* that FairPay offer an adaptive FairPay premium-level strategy that is far more promising. Much as explained before:

- The *Times* identifies me as a current digital and print subscriber, and offers to let me try *Premier* on a FairPay basis, as a "patron" of their quality journalism.
- They "bill" me in arrears on a pay what you want (PWYW) basis, telling me for the past four weeks how much of each

Premier feature I used, and advising me of a suggested price based on that usage and my history. The suggested price may reflect volume discounts and a maximum for "unlimited" use, and may have adjustments for students, disadvantaged, or affluent patrons.

- They try to nudge me to pay well by reminding me of their quality journalism, telling me that others are paying much as they suggest, and offering added incentives.
- I decide whether I think it is fair to pay as suggested, higher, or lower, and check off possible reasons for that.
- The *Times* weighs the reasons, considers my history, demographics, and usage, and decides how fair my price seems—on an individualized basis.
- After a period of learning, the *Times* decides whether to continue as is, bump me up to more privileged offers, or drop me from FairPay pricing and require that I pay the standard $10 per cycle if I want to continue *Premier/Insider*.
- This dynamic adaptation continues indefinitely, as the product and the relationship change and evolve.

This has the usual benefits of FairPay to both me and the *Times*:

- It lets me try *Premier* at no risk (the *Times* could suggest that I am expected to pay, even for the first four weeks, but only if I do find value in it).
- Each cycle, I can pay as suggested, based on my usage—or more or less—as I think fair.
- If I have an occasional heavy usage cycle, I can apply whatever "volume discount" I think fair to avoid an unduly high charge, as long as I don't abuse that privilege.
- If I thought that the features were especially good that cycle, I can pay a bit more, which would increase my fairness rating to show my "patronship"—and earn more privileges.
- If I thought that the features were less good that cycle, I can pay less, and only harm my reputation and privileges if I make a habit of devaluing the product.

Some of the key benefits to *The Times*

- They can get far more people to try *Premier/Insider*, and retain far more, for wider market reach and greater profit. Many may pay less than the standard $10, but some may pay more, generally in line with the value they receive. The net profit can be higher—with a lower average price, but from more patrons (and with more advertising views).
- When *Premier* was a new offering, they would not risk cannibalizing existing revenues. Even now, an added FairPay option could extend its reach down-market, and add more premium revenue up-market.
- They can build a deeper relationship with their patrons, based on this deeper empowerment, dialog, and experience.
- That can shift the relationship with the *Times* from quid-pro-quo business exchange norms to cooperative, communal norms, and foster social values of fairness and reciprocity, both of which increase willingness to pay.
- They can learn far more about what their patrons value and why.
- They can justify different prices to patrons with different value propositions and abilities to pay.
- They can start with fairly simple decision rules and liberal continuation criteria, and gradually add more nuance and discrimination as they and their patrons gain experience with the process.

Trying a radically new approach like FairPay has risks, and takes some effort, but I suggest that a FairPay version of *Times Premier/Insider* offers far more profit potential and far better relationships with the *Times'* patrons than the conventional version.

More generally, FairPay promises to be a particularly effective way to set pricing for rewards in loyalty programs, such as those based on points or miles (as noted in Chapter 7). Instead of set prices in points, why not FairPay dialogs? What better way to more deeply engage customers who already show loyalty and appreciation of your services? To limit risk, initial trials can begin with selected customers, and selected classes of rewards that have low marginal cost.

Testing FairPay for New Customer Acquisition

Why not start FairPay trials at the beginning, with new customers? This can be done quietly, on a very selective basis—such as to prospects thought to have strong social values of fairness, and likely to value the service, even if their willingness to pay is unclear. This can be positioned as a special trial that will end if not enough customers play the game in a way that works.

Instead of a free trial period, as is usual with many subscription services, with FairPay it can be framed that payment is expected as soon as you see value. Maybe with a trial discount to compensate for your forebearance for a while, but why should it be free if you do see value? Some population of new customers could be onboarded to this special trial, and given 6 to 12 months to see how this works. How much can be learned?—and what harm if results are not good?

Transitioning from Free or Ad-Supported to FairPay

If paid subscriptions are not yet in place, why not try this segue? While many businesses have bit the bullet and transitioned from free or ad-supported to paid subscriptions, it is often the case that many consumers will balk. One way to ease this transition is to use FairPay as a way to offer a kinder, gentler paywall—and combine that with the bonus of going ad-free (or at least reducing the ad load). This benefits both the business, and customers:

- Customers feel more respected and empowered by the added trust and flexibility.
- Customers might get ad-free basic content, at some modest cost, presumably less than the likely paywall rate.
- Some will pay less for the premium content, but some will pay more.
- Relating pricing to usage can get heavy viewers to pay more, compensating for those who pay (and use) less.
- Many who might refuse a conventional set-price premium service might be willing to pay something reasonable for a FairPay basic service—added revenue.

- The details of the offers and the process can be individually and dynamically tuned to encourage good payment levels, and to send free-riders back into the hard paywall.

Bottom line: more happy customers; more revenue.

FairPay "Free Trial" or "Survey" Mode
Easing into FairPay, and Understanding Your Customers

Looking at the details of phasing in the FairPay process itself, there are ways to do that in steps that maximize joint learning with your customers and defer much of the software development until you gain some confidence.

The idea is to get some basic dialogs about value started at low cost—and to learn more about your customers, so you can better manage your investment and your risk (and improve your business overall). Whether for an entirely new business, or for a new pricing approach in an established business:

- Key questions about FairPay are how hard is it to integrate with your pricing systems, and to what extent might it put revenue at risk.
- Key benefits of FairPay are as a learning process, centered on dialog with your customers, about what they want from you, and how they value it.

This can not only be applied in existing businesses, but is also especially suited to new lines of business where the value proposition may be uncertain or temporarily limited (such as beta tests, pilots, etc.). Limitations may be due to lack of system function or lack of critical mass network effects, such as those affecting content richness, community participation, and so on. This can also apply to a shift from ad-support to customer-supported subscriptions, as described earlier.

FairPay Free Trial Mode: Initially, *FairPay Free Trial Mode* should stay largely out of the way, behaving generally as a conventional "free trial," with the addition of some key features:

- *The initial objective* is to serve as a learning platform, apart from any revenue generation, to obtain customer "survey" data related to the potential value of the service. This role can integrate with other customer feedback to focus on the perceived value exchange, to better understand the benefits and problems in using the service by the consumer.

- From this perspective, *FairPay Free Trial Mode* can be thought of equally as a *FairPay Survey Mode*, in which data on willingness to pay is collected, but is not used to limit continuing use, even if users do not pay. Depending on the situation—or in successive phases—users might be asked:

  1. *No-Payment Survey Mode: to simply say what they "would" be willing to pay* without actually making any payment.

  2. *Real-Payment Survey Mode: to actually pay what they think fair*, with the understanding that all *payments are entirely voluntary* (pure PWYW, in arrears, "pay as you exit")—there are no adverse consequences (no reputational harm) for nonpayment.

- *A secondary objective* is to set the stage for *Full FairPay (Fairness-Gated) Mode* use to follow, by facilitating learning by both customers and the service provider on how FairPay is best applied to the particular services. This would educate customers on basic concepts of the FairPay process, and help the service provider learn where to apply FairPay, how to frame offers, how to suggest prices and assess fairness, and the like, in the context of their particular services and customer base.

- To aid in customer understanding, it might be clearly stated that FairPay is currently in *Free Trial Mode* for some or all services, and that a future transition to *Full FairPay Mode* was planned.

These modes can be enabled before a full FairPay system infrastructure is built, since they require none of the real-time feedback analysis, buyer fairness reputation rating, and reputation-based offer gating of a full FairPay service. Thus these partial steps toward FairPay require very minimal development investment.

Full FairPay (Fairness-Gated) Mode: As the service matures, the *Full FairPay (Fairness-Gated) Mode* can be implemented and gradually turned on—with any desired phasing as to customer segments and service categories. *Full FairPay Mode* would enforce FairPay "fairness-gating"—limiting access by buyers who develop a reputation for failing to pay fairly. This can overlap with continuing use of *FairPay Trial Mode* for other customers and other service categories.

- The shift to *FairPay Fairness-Gated Mode* might be related to achieving a level of maturity as to service robustness, critical mass scale (in content and community), initial education of customers on FairPay concepts—and to scale-driven needs for revenue.
- This shift can be phased in (sector-by-sector, if desired), using an appropriate change management process. Customer communications and dialog can be applied to prepare customers for this change (to include customer reputation rating and gating of offers), to identify any issues or concerns and ensure that they are recognized and addressed. It would be made clear to users that gating was being activated, why the time for that was right, and what changes to expect.

The result of this staging approach is that FairPay can begin quickly to create a lightweight dialog with customers about value, and to generate valuable data long before it is integrated into actual payment processes. That imposes minimal burden on customers, and also allows the development work of building the full FairPay infrastructure to be phased with careful controls.

CHAPTER 15

Increasing Sophistication and Variety

While we are at the early days of FairPay (and any similarly adaptive, relationship-oriented methods), it is helpful to keep in mind where this might go. That not only adds to the motivation, but helps put early steps into perspective. This split between what are early opportunities and what is more advanced is merely an initial projection, and there may be surprises along the road. Designing for flexibility and adaptability is central to this strategy.

Adaptation of the Adaptation Process—Parameterized Architectures and Policies

It is important to understand the power of FairPay as an *architecture*—it is not a single structure or method or algorithm, but a framework that provides for infinite variation and inherent agility.

People often ask how FairPay works in some particular detail, and I answer that I think that in many situations it is best done in some particular way, for some particular reasons—but that it could be done differently. Until we do testing in a particular context, controlling for other variables, it is hard to know just what form of FairPay will be most effective for that use-case.

Referring back to the operational details section, the only criterion that I would view as essential to properly being what I call "FairPay" is the core FairPay cycle (the invisible handshake): That is the fundamental mechanism of balancing customer post-pricing power (price it backwards) with business power to control what further offers are made (extend it forward?). All else is implementation detail.

So we can view FairPay itself as *an adaptive process for finding the right adaptive process* to achieve win–win customer relationships in any given context. It consists of a basic architecture that structures the FairPay cycle using various policy options, parameters, and rules. Everything is parameterized, with a hierarchy of algorithms, rules, and thresholds. Any given set of policies or rules can then be used to adaptively seek win–win prices. But at a higher level we can vary the rules and policies themselves as *parameters* to find combinations that are more effective in a given situation. So all of this is an ongoing multivariate adaptation process. *That can also apply beyond what might be considered FairPay itself to optimize the hybrid mix of FairPay and other policies, working together in an adaptively win–win system of commerce.*

This relies on a continuous process of experimentation—from early trials of FairPay, to rich expansions of advanced versions of FairPay, conventional methods, hybrids, and new methods we have not yet added to the mix. Again, this experimentation is not a special side-process that leads to some aspect to then be baked in, but a process of continuous experimentation and adaptation that is inherent in every customer journey. So we should keep in mind that we cannot be sure what variations to test, and may learn that we need to change the mix. As this develops, we can add increasing layers of richness and nuance.

A parameterized policy framework is online at FPZLink, but that is just a first iteration, to be adapted and expanded. The major categories of parameters listed are as follows:

1. Mostly generic to all pay what you want (PWYW) and FairPay
   - Offer selectivity—segmentation criteria (with or without FairPay fairness reputation).
   - Timing of pricing (post or ante) by transaction stage (combine with specific pricing rights).
   - Buyer pricing rights applicable at each stage (post or ante).
   - PWYW pricing constraints (more constraint signals less trust and might reduce generosity).
   - Reference/anchor prices.
   - Offer tiers/carrots/sticks and gamification.
   - Product/service offer range/segmentation/tiers.

2. Mostly specific to FairPay
   - Framing opportunities along the customer journey—which touchpoints/which messages.
   - Framing strategies—overall positioning of "invisible hand-shake" between buyer and seller.
   - Fairness rating parameters.
   - Offer/relationship continuation policies.
   - Repeated game horizon control (quasi-infinite or bounded).
   - Value verification methods.
   - Pricing touchpoints, frequency—FairPay credit extended by seller, autopilot for buyer.

There is also a dimension of algorithmic sophistication and nuance that fleshes out this structure. These rules and policies relate to learning processes about customers and how they price for what. Early implementations can use simple quantitative rules, factors, and thresholds, while more advanced ones can use a variety of advanced statistical and machine learning and prediction techniques to optimize each rule or policy as they are applied individually and in combination. I am not expert in such techniques, but sophisticated marketing analysts already apply a rich and growing arsenal of such methods.

This richness should be viewed not as a problem, but as an opportunity—to start simply, begin to learn what works, find alternatives when things don't quite work, then continue an ongoing process of adding more sophistication and nuance. Any initial failures should not be taken as final, only as signals to alter course appropriately.

Adaptively Seeking Needs to Serve—Personalized Packaging and Product Design

As a further dimension, FairPay provides rich feedback on value propositions that can be used not only for price setting, but also for continuously adaptive redesign of the broader aspects of value proposition—what is the product or the product package?

It has been clear since Alvin Toffler's *Future Shock* (1970) that our economy provides increasingly rich capabilities to mass customize products. We have long seen this in simple form in digital products that are personalized, and it is becoming increasingly the case for physical products. Automobile options were an early case in point, and now 3-D manufacturing takes this much farther.

So far this has been based on conventional marketing data about the consumer and their desires, but the value feedback of FairPay will add *a new perspective on individual consumer preferences and the value placed on them by each consumer.* This value-weighting of preferences will in time enable mass customization to be value-optimized. Not just mass-personalization of prices, but *dynamic mass-personalization and co-design of all aspects of value-proposition*s. That will lead to even greater productivity, efficiency, and growth.

CHAPTER 16

Proving the Concept

The concept of FairPay has received very positive response, but has been in the development phase until now, and is not yet widely known—hence the purpose of this book. The next step is to undertake definitive proof of concept testing in practice. There has been strong interest from senior executives in a diversity of content and platform companies, entrepreneurs, and prominent scholars. The component strategies are proven, and this new combination is seen to be sensible, promising, and even revolutionary. The hurdles are not large—once proof of concept tests are in hand, progress can be expected to be very rapid.

What are the hurdles facing enterprises as they consider moving in this direction? (More at FPZLink.)

Trial Investment:

- Software: The phased approach suggested in Chapter 14 can limit the initial investment, and extensive materials on the high-level program design are online, but the software for tracking fairness and gating offers will take some coding. Getting a simple but fully gated level of FairPay into a limited trial might take on the order of several man-months of software development, as corroborated by independent experts.
- Business analysis: The design of how a trial fits into a business and the evaluation of test findings will also take some work. That also might require several man-months of analysis, as corroborated by independent experts. Several of my academic collaborators have proposed to work as a team to assist in design and analysis of trials, and other researchers have also expressed interest in assisting in this ground-breaking work.
- Business risk: As explained earlier, trials can be confined to small test populations and framed as experiments—to

minimize revenue at risk and any broader business risk. While some may be tempted to wait and be fast followers, there are first mover advantages. FairPay trials could also have very powerful public relations value—with test subjects and more broadly.

Customer Response:

- Learning curve: This radical shift in thinking about business relationships will take some customer (and business) education, and will involve a learning curve. Care should be taken to manage the education process to ensure good results, and to avoid mistaking correctible failures in customer selection, education, and acclimatization as flaws that are inherent in the FairPay strategy.
- Cognitive burden: There may be some cognitive burden to the dialogs on value and pricing actions, but ease in restaurant tipping suggests that this problem is very tractable with effective choice architectures, and can become quite simple after the initial learning curve.
- Fairness: Some customers may view personalized pricing as unfair, and some may seek to game the system to pay the least permissible. That can be minimized and contained by effective market segmentation, transparent explanation of the justification for individual variations, and simple validation of customer value feedback against measured usage data.

The most important strategy is to focus on lines of business and customer segments that promise to be initial sweet spots. FairPay represents a consumer behavior change (even if that is back toward a more natural, cooperative kind of relationship). As outlined in Chapter 14, the sweet spots will be segments that are disposed to high fairness and generosity (such as superfans getting much-appreciated service from deserving providers) and that are willing to invest some effort to be responsible about sharing pricing power. Once the power of FairPay is demonstrated in such sweet spots (even if restricted to a minority of customers), broader expansion will become more and more compelling to both customers and firms.

In summary, FairPay is radical paradigm shift for both businesses and consumers that will take some time and effort, but promises rich rewards, and solutions to increasingly urgent problems.

- It relies on a new synergy to drive situational behaviors of fairness, trust, and transparency that have become unconventional in customer relationships, but are clearly natural, and had been a common norm.
- The payoffs promise to be very large, and urgently needed, and the initial hurdles are very manageable. Its full power will take time to develop, but it promises to offer immediate benefits in important markets.
- Enterprises should seek to understand this new direction and how it applies to their business, and think about how best to start on a managed path to better, more adaptively win–win, customer relationships.

PART III
Needs and Perspectives

CHAPTER 17

Practical Business Comparison to Conventional Methods

A Recap of Notable Pricing Strategies

Current strategies are failing us, and FairPay promises a more win–win solution. Here we consider a selection of pricing methods that are in wide use, plus some less common alternatives that have interesting features.

A fundamental problem of all conventional methods is that they do not price effectively for a value that varies from person to person and from time to time. For example:

- Unlimited or "all you can eat" (AYCE) underprices to heavy users, and overprices to light users.
- Set prices of any kind underprice to those who most value an item or are most able to afford it, and overprice to those who find limited value or have limited means.

This results in a deadweight loss to our economy—a loss to society. The set price excludes the large numbers of potential customers who would gladly pay less, and thus would (1) obtain value, and (2) contribute a profit to the seller. This is *partly* a matter of usage volume. Pricing for usage has always been a problem (think of long-distance phone bills and cellular data), but now it is far more widespread and problematic for products and services that involve significant costs of human creation but low cost of replication. AYCE is especially painful to the creators of content (musicians and authors) who find themselves getting pennies for their hard-earned work (as has been much in the news for services such as Spotify and Amazon Unlimited).

Table 17.1 compares some notable pricing strategies (the rows) for five important attributes that have been discussed throughout this book (the columns). For each attribute, there are one to five squares, intended to serve as a visual bar graph that is suggestive of the strength of that strategy with regard to that attribute (in fuzzy terms, and of course dependent on particular situations). Some background on each of those strategies follows in Table 17.2.

The attributes are:

- Post-pricing (versus ante-pricing)—All are ante-pricing in more or less pure form except for some of the participative alternatives (see the further explanation that follows the table);
- Customer participation—Most widely accepted strategies allow no customer participation in setting prices (other than buying a given volume/selection or not). The participative alternatives offer participation that can range from shared with the seller to full control by the buyer (Bertini and Koenigsberg 2014);
- Perceived value tracking—The extent to which a customer is likely to feel that the price paid corresponds to the value received. As discussed, this is essential to effective pricing;
- Relationship/loyalty—The extent to which the pricing strategy is likely to help build a meaningful relationship and feelings of loyalty from customers, including perceived value tracking, and other factors, such as a sense of partnership, responsiveness, and control; and
- Commercial acceptance—The current level of use by businesses, especially in markets for digital services (but also other experience goods/services). (Empty squares are shown for value-based pricing to reflect that it is well accepted in B2B markets, but generally not applied to B2C markets.)

This chart shows the significant weaknesses of most conventional methods, and the appeal of the alternatives. It also shows how FairPay promises to be superior in all of these attributes.

Table 17.1 Pricing strategy comparison

Pricing strategy	Post-pricing (vs. ante-)	Customer participation	Perceived value tracking	Relationship/ loyalty	Commercial acceptance
Subscription-oriented					
Freemium subscription (AYCE)	■	■	■■	■■	■■■■■
Tiered subscription (multiple price levels)	■	■	■■■	■■	■■■
Hard paywall subscription (AYCE)	■	■	■	■	■■■
Usage-priced subscription—flat per unit	■■	■	■■	■	■■■
Usage-priced subscription—volume discount	■■	■	■■■	■■	■■■
Bundled subscription—pre-bundled	■	■	■■■	■■	■■■
Bundled subscription—post-bundled (new)	■■■	■	■■■■	■■■	??
Item-oriented					
Item unit sale—flat	■	■	■■	■	■■■■■
Item unit sale—volume discount	■■	■	■■■	■■	■■■
Item unit sale—bundled	■	■	■■■	■■	■■■
Item unit sale—personalized by seller	■■	■	■■	■?	■■
Micropayments	■■	■	■■	■■	■■
Participative alternatives					
Pay what you want (PWYW)—ante	■	■■■■	■■	■■	■
PWYW—post	■■■■■	■■■■■	■■■■■	■■■	■
Value-based	■■■■	■■■	■■■■■	■■■■	□□□□
FairPay (new)	■■■■■	■■■■	■■■■■	■■■■■	????

To clarify post-pricing, it can be viewed as relating to a spectrum of degrees of "late binding" of price to usage, as determined after the fact. The essential aspect of post-pricing is that the price rate schedule is not pre-set, but determined after use.

- *Pure ante-pricing* sets all aspects of price up-front, such as with AYCE subscriptions or simple item pricing.
- *Simple usage pricing* is a form of ante-pricing that has some dependency on actual usage—the price *rate* per item is still set in advance, but the price *total* depends on the number of units used.
- *Volume-discounted usage pricing* is still ante-pricing, in that the price *rate schedule* is pre-set, but the applicable unit rate depends on the actual volume used.
- *Pre-bundling or package pricing* is a variation on volume discounting, with the bundles or packages pre-defined by the seller (possibly with a menu of options).
- *Post-bundling* (as proposed in other chapters), applies pre-set bundle/package rates to packages that are composed by the customer on-demand, and then totaled after the fact based on pre-set bundling discount rates.
- *True post-pricing*, as used in this book, occurs when the price *rate*, itself, is set after the usage, thus including all of the degrees of freedom just listed, plus the ability to adjust the rates, themselves, after the fact.

Post-pricing is late binding, in that it is a form of real options strategy—it delays the pricing decision, and thus enables better tracking to value as realized in use. Late binding can reduce predictability—so when done just partially, and without adequate customer transparency and control, it can lead to unpleasant surprises. That can be a consumer acceptance/fairness issue, such as with simple usage pricing, and to a lesser degree, with volume or package discounts. But when done with customer participation (plus seller protections), as with FairPay, it can most closely approximate win–win value setting.

Table 17.2 adds some commentary on each of the pricing methods in Table 17.1.

Much additional background on most of these strategies and how they compare to FairPay is in other chapters, and more is online (see FPZLink). This chapter concludes with some further discussion of freemium (and we delve deeper into PWYW in Chapter 20).

Table 17.2 Pricing strategy commentary

Subscription-oriented
Freemium subscription (AYCE) (paywalls)
AYCE at a set price, time-limited, split between a limited free tier, and a paid tier, usually just one. This has become very popular as perhaps the best solution readily available for many digital services, such as Spotify, newspapers (metered or "soft" paywalls), and many others. But freemium is still a form of AYCE, with all its inefficiency, and it still has a set price, so the challenge of what price, at what level, remains (see FPZLink).
Tiered subscription (multiple price levels)
Tiers add some correspondence to value, to better segment the market, but still the tiers and prices are pre-set, and do not adapt to the fact that value varies in many dimensions other than just quantity of usage.
Hard paywall subscription (AYCE)
This is the original form of subscription, prior to freemium, and is still widely used. The correlation to value for light users discourages use to the point of hostility to that segment.
Usage-priced subscription—flat per unit
Unit-pricing in subscriptions was common for communications services (voice, mobile, data) but tracks so unpredictably to perceived value (fear of the "ticking meter") that it has largely given way to other strategies (notably volume discount or AYCE).
Usage-priced subscription—volume discount
This improves on flat unit rates (and reduces fear of the "ticking meter"), and is now common for many communications services.
Bundled subscriptions—pre-bundled
Similar to a volume discount, but for seller-constructed bundles (packages), common for cable TV channel bundles.
Bundled subscriptions—post-bundled (new)
A variant I have proposed—a simple combination of bundling discounts, based on pre-set volume discounts but computed after the fact, based on actual usage. For example, a cable TV offering priced at a bundled rate, for whatever mix of channels/programs was viewed that month (see FPZLink).
Item-oriented
Item unit sale—flat
Essentially AYCE at a set price, of a single item, forever. This is simple and easy, and works for those who want to make full use of a given item (song, book, video, app, etc.), but tends to make it prohibitive to use very many different items less fully.

(Continued)

(Continued)

Item unit sale—volume discount Volume discounts generally improve the correspondence to perceived value, and encourage increased purchases.
Item unit sale—bundled Similar to a volume discount, but for seller-constructed bundles (packages), common for software and games (and of course music albums are bundles of tracks).
Item unit sale—personalized by seller Seller-side personalization (dynamic pricing) can track better to value as the seller understands it, but is generally poorly received by customers, as being non-transparent, discriminatory, and exploitive.
Micropayments Small set prices for each small unit. This variant of usage-related pricing has a long history of conceptual appeal and repeated attempts, but is unforgiving, with the fear of the "ticking meter," and typically does not provide volume discounts.
Participative alternatives
PWYW—ante (or Tipjar/Microdonation) This has proven successful in some markets such as indie music, games, and e-books. While it has been well established that most people will pay, and many will pay fairly or even generously, it is still very iffy as a sustainable business model. Its success so far has been greatest in special promotions. (A limiting factor has been the single transaction setting, unlike FairPay.)
PWYW—post (or Tipjar/Microdonation) Post-pricing has been little used, but has a big advantage in that it encourages the customer to set a more generous price because they need not fear disappointment—and it signals greater trust and confidence from the seller, to further encourage generous pricing. (One older variant is shareware, but with a choice between a set price or zero. Again a limiting factor has been the single transaction setting.)
Value-based (performance-based, outcomes-based) Collaborative post-pricing based on actual results of use, using pre-agreed criteria—Near the ideal of pricing for value with perfect price discrimination. As currently done, this has been impractical in consumer markets, but it has proven (Shapiro 2002) very effective and efficient in B2B, where the parties can agree on how to measure value and share in the value surplus that the product/service creates, and can do the analysis that takes. Big Data is making this more feasible and effective (Iansiti and Lakhani 2014) in a wider variety of businesses.
FairPay (new) As explained here—participative post-pricing with a balance of buyer and seller powers, over a relationship (thus unlike PWYW). Applicable to both subscriptions and item sales. It adapts to the fact that value is not just how much you eat, of what and when, but how good is it—a particular and ever-changing mix of how tasty, exciting, nutritious, timely, sustaining, and so on.

Beyond Freemium

Freemium AYCE subscription is increasingly the dominant model in digital services for consumers, because it has been seen to best address the challenges of free replication and expensive creation. Its combination of a free tier and a premium tier (*free* + pre*mium*) has proven more successful than most prior strategies across a wide range of businesses—as was well described in the 2009 book *Free* by Chris Anderson (Anderson 2009).

But, while freemium works better for digital, it still has fundamental issues. *With regard to the problem of inefficient set prices, freemium just kicks the can down the road a bit, without really solving the problem.* A business still has to decide where to set the boundary between free and paid, and what price to set for paid. That is impossible to do efficiently across a wide range of customers—and even optimizing that on average is no easy task.

FairPay takes the driving objective of freemium—exploiting "free" to move toward a profitable relationship over time—and *makes that the driver of a dynamically variable boundary between free and paid tiers.* Fair-Pay moves the strategic question of what to exchange at what price from a pre-set seller decision to an emergent, dynamic process that balances the interests of the seller and each individual buyer. That provides more nuance and flexibility than freemium's gross segmentation into just two (or a very few) set tiers (free or paid).

"Making 'Freemium' Work" by Vineet Kumar in Harvard Business Review (May 2014), nicely sheds light on companies' real-world experience with freemium. It highlights the challenges of making it work, and suggests how companies can tune it to get good results. Building on that, we consider how the more individually adaptive techniques of FairPay can be applied to get better market reach and profit, and to build deeper and more profitable long-term relationships. Kumar poses six questions as being critical to making freemium work effectively. FairPay provides a systematic method for answering all of them—by applying a very different logic.

1. *What should be free?* With freemium, this is a very visible static parameter that is hard to guess right, and hard to change. With Fair-Pay, the boundary is soft and dynamically individualized.

2. *Do customers fully understand the premium offer?* FairPay is built around a structured dialog about offers and value received, and lets customers in good standing *try* both basic and premium offers whenever they want, and *then* determine the value they see in it. The process is structured, but lightweight, informal, dynamic, and intuitive.

3. *What is your target conversion rate?* Freemium centers on a single all-or-nothing boundary between free and paid. That makes it costly to guess wrong, and either miss much of the market or leave money on the table (by undercharging good customers). With FairPay, "free" users are permitted to pay zero percent of suggested price, while paying users can pay whatever seems fair—the conversion process is one of nudging customers up the pricing curve, and getting them to try (and pay for) more valuable features. This dynamic multivariate optimization process is more complex, but even simple heuristics can offer far more nuance and flexibility than the hard boundary of freemium.

4. *Are you prepared for the conversion life cycle?* Early adopters are less price-sensitive than others, and are often people for whom the value proposition is unusually compelling. Freemium has no way to adapt to such variations over time, except to move the boundary for everyone. The core process of FairPay is driven by ongoing dynamic adaptation to different price-sensitivities and value perceptions.

5. *Are users becoming evangelists?* Free users can have value as evangelists and also as a target for advertising (a key revenue source for many services), and viral marketing can be very important. FairPay can please customers all along the Long Tail of Customers, not just the free tier, so that they share that with others, and it can also attract large numbers of price-sensitive customers to accept ad-viewing as a way to compensate for a low subscription price.

6. *Are you committed to ongoing innovation?* Freemium is very focused on customer acquisition, but does little to address retention. FairPay is designed to do its adaptive work throughout the life cycle, as usage

and understanding of the product matures and changes over time. It sets prices dynamically, in accord with current perceived value, and continually drives the seller to make more desirable offers, based on detailed, real-world customer preference data. Retention is always inherent to that.

This chapter seeks to briefly contrast the new logic of FairPay to conventional methods, complementing discussion in other chapters. If additional grounding in prior methods and the general issues of pricing in the digital era is desired, two works are suggested. Extensive coverage of freemium and how to manage it is provided in Seufert (2014). A broad grounding in the basic principles of the network economy is provided in Shapiro and Varian (1999).

CHAPTER 18

Customer-Hostile Value Propositions

The inherent inefficiency and unfairness of conventional pricing methods and the business relationships built around them have been noted throughout this book. Mostly, this unfairness is unintentional, a matter of inattention, and the inherent unfairness of set-price methods (whether all you can eat or usage-based). In this chapter, we highlight a few common business practices where that neglect verges on downright customer-hostility.

The point here is not simply that FairPay offers a better strategy, but the larger idea that much of current business thinking is simply blind to the importance of seeking win–win value propositions, even when that would be easy. Consumers have an intuitive sense of value, and a revulsion for pricing policies that appear to go against the grain of value. Businesses would do well to be more attuned to the customer perspective on value, especially to avoid cases of flagrant disregard. (More at FPZLink.)

Artificial Scarcity, Copyright, and the Death of Piracy

Perhaps most fundamentally counterproductive and customer-hostile is the idea of artificial scarcity. As many content producers view it, the inherent wonder of digital, its lack of scarcity, is a not a benefit, but a curse. Never mind that there is much value to be shared very widely with effective pricing. The old logic is that scarcity drives high prices, and so publishers should use every trick in the book to create a degree of artificial scarcity—hard paywalls and price fencing, protected by strict and expansive copyright enforcement—even to the point of suing individual consumers for piracy (which even the music industry reluctantly came to recognize as counterproductive)!

Perhaps the biggest blow up in recent years was in 2012, when publishers succeeded in lobbying the U.S. Congress to vote on two bills that would dramatically extend the power of copyright owners while putting draconian restrictions on consumers. At the 11th hour, the tech lobby rallied massive consumer protests to cause the resounding defeat of these bills, called the Protect IP Act (PIPA) and the Stop Online Piracy Act (SOPA). FairPay puts this issue into interesting perspective. It suggests that the way to end piracy is not to reduce the supply, but to reduce the demand for piracy.

What is the real objective here? Copyright and ownership of intellectual property are not ends in themselves, but means to a larger end. This larger end, is clear in the Constitution: "To promote the Progress of Science and useful Arts, by securing for limited Times to Authors and Inventors the exclusive Right to their respective Writings and Discoveries."

- Thus copyright is clearly only a means "to promote the Progress of Science and useful Arts."
- It would be foolish to apply measures to protect copyright that impede "the Progress of Science and useful Arts" more than they promote it.

The problem with PIPA and SOPA is that they seem to overstep the objective, and to enhance a *means* at potentially high cost to the desired *end*. There are two real issues:

- The Internet has facilitated piracy to the point that it threatens the ability of creators of writings and other arts to earn reasonable compensation for their work, and thus threatens the progress we seek for society. If creators lack fair compensation, fewer will create, and society will lose.
- We (society) support IP ownership to the extent that it is good for society, not for its own sake.

The challenge is to find better ways to ensure the fair compensation of creators for the good of society. The Internet is a tidal change—we must learn to channel the tide, and harness it, not try to stop it.

Fairness and Piracy

Robert Levine's book, "Free Ride," (Levine 2011) provides a nice summary of many of the issues of piracy, and makes it clear that some level of piracy is inevitable, with a level that depends on a number of factors, including:

1. The ease and effectiveness of piracy relative to any issues of quality and risk.
2. The ease and effectiveness of legitimate sources.
3. The cost of legitimate access (relative to piracy).
4. Social and ethical factors relating to the legitimacy of the IP owner, and the fairness of stealing from them (stealing service, not bits).

It is well known that the Internet has shifted at least #1 and #4 toward piracy.

The real solution is not laws and other efforts to shift #1 (although some modest improvement may be gained), but to shift #2 to 4, and especially #4. The value of shifting #2 and #3 are well known, and summarized by Levine. What is less recognized is how important #4, fairness, is.

FairPay can help kill piracy by letting buyers pay what they think fair, within limits.

- When buyers can buy legitimately for a price they accept as fair, the cost becomes a non-issue. Those who have limited means or get little value can still buy for a price that considers those factors fairly.
- When buyers can buy legitimately for a price they accept as fair, the fairness of piracy becomes clearly insupportable for all but the sociopathic. It is hard to argue that "information wants to be free" (as in free beer), when it is *free enough*.

Piracy is a tax imposed by the people on the sellers of IP—a Robin Hood tax. When the price of content seems onerous, people feel that they should not have to pay for it, and piracy appears justified. It is seen as noble for the poor to steal from the oppressive rich.

Killing the Demand for Piracy, Not the Supply

As with any illegitimate product, it is generally easier and more effective to reduce demand, not to choke off supply. That is best done not by legislation, but by making the legitimate alternative more attractive. (How iTunes killed Napster is a well-known case in point.)

There are a number of interrelated levers to move in that direction:

- FairPay pricing is a significant step in the right direction. It makes prices more suited to individual buyer's needs, values, and ability to pay. Copyright owners retain the right to extract their "monopoly rents," but must balance that with the quid pro quo of society's desire to benefit from their creations.
- Making sellers more legitimate in the eyes of customers is also a major factor. To the extent the IP owners are seen as evil, faceless corporations that exploit their customers (and their creators), it is easy to justify stealing from them. Showing that they listen to customers and can be flexible in pricing will greatly increase their perceived legitimacy and deservedness.
- Getting sellers to be more clearly respectful of creators can also have a big effect. Many music labels are perceived as sharing little of their profit with their artists. While they do have real costs of nurturing, marketing, and managing, clearly the Internet is shifting that toward "skinnier" models. Middlemen must either get skinny, or demonstrate why they deserve the share they get, and be transparent about how much they share with the creators.

FairPay is not essential to all these levers, but it can contribute significantly to all of them.

When buyers set prices, no man will be a pirate. That may not be true in every case, but in enough.

Ad-Blocking—Kicking and Screaming to Win–Win Value Propositions

Ad-blocking is a newer cause-celeb—to publishers, ad-blocking looms much like piracy, as an existential threat (especially since Apple enabled it for mobile). But this may just force the end of an era of customer abuse deservedly left behind.

Things are so bad that the industry recognizes it must change. As described in the PageFair and Adobe 2015 Ad Blocking Report (PageFair 2015), which estimates that loss of global revenue due to blocked advertising during that year was $21.8B:

> ... ad blocking is endemic only because online advertising has become so invasive that hundreds of millions of people are willing to take matters into their own hands. To sustainably solve ad blocking, we must treat these users with respect, not force feed them the popovers, interstitials and video ads that they are trying to get rid of.

Publishers have relied on ads to pay the freight, so customers could buy their content at low rates. Some sites even have terms of service that make the contract explicit—you agree to view our ads in exchange for access to our content. As with piracy, legal attacks on ad-blocking are being considered by some.

But there is growing recognition that the real problem is that the advertising value proposition has become a bad one. Publishers have chosen to give customers no choice, but now the ad-blockers have taken the decision out of their hands. Steps toward changing this are emerging—the PageFair/Adobe report goes on to say:

> Sites which sign up for PageFair are given an analytics system precisely aimed at determining how many visitors are blocking ads, as well as a supplemental advertising system that displays adverts to adblockers only. The idea is that Web sites use those supplemental ads to ask visitors to turn off ad blocking software, appealing to their better nature and laying out the economic difficulty with operating in an environment where ad blocking is commonplace.

Any move in that direction will bring publishers closer to still more cooperative models such as FairPay. FairPay prices can be based on a new kind of value metering that acts as a flexible guide, not an oppressive sledgehammer. And it can be a value meter that runs in both directions—charges for value received, and credits for value given (such as in the form of ad-viewing, personal data that can be sold, viral promotion, user-generated content, etc.). All this is based on a win–win balance of powers. The Internet has leveled the playing field, and the sooner suppliers recognize that, the better for all of us.

Post-Bundling—Packaging Better Value Propositions with 20–20 Hindsight

The TV/video industry has been sheltered from the tides of digital a bit longer than music and journalism, but they are under increasing pressure, and their increasingly challenged practice of bundling channels into subscriptions suggests broader lessons. The shift from bundles of cable TV channels to Internet-based "Over the Top" (OTT) and "*a la carte*"—or at least "skinny bundles" or reconfigurable bundles—has raised cheers and fears—and an industry stock market decline (Hufford 2015). But we should be thinking about a more win–win kind of "post-bundling" future.

Once again, we take pre-set cable TV bundles for granted, as the way things are, but think about it. What sense does it make for me to choose ahead of time what channels I want to be able to watch in a given month (from a menu with only a limited choice of bundles)? Does Spotify ask me to choose what record labels I will want to listen to? How would I know?

There is a very simple way to do much better (even without FairPay tracking and feedback processes). Let viewers pay for what they use, and do it in a sensible way that corresponds to that. Current bundles (regular or skinny) do not do that, a la carte does not do that (not without discounts), and flat-rate video on demand does not do that. Viewing is irregular and unpredictable—the only way to determine its value is after it is logged.

Instead of selecting a bundle from a menu beforehand, we should be able to consume dim sum-style, track what we used, *and then have the seller price that under an appropriate discount schedule* (unlike simple dim sum). A simplistic undiscounted dim sum at a la carte prices would be overpriced, and customers will fear running up high charges. Conventional video on demand (when available) is based on undiscounted pay-per-view pricing—but doing more than occasional viewing this way gets very expensive fast. It is easy to do better, with discount tiers for various levels of viewing, and for various mixes of premium content.

- Pricing should factor in not only which channels were viewed, but how many shows (and maybe even which ones).
- Tiered plans could give average per-program prices similar to current bundles, but with the flexibility to dynamically alter the composition of the bundle.
- Usage factors could reasonably be set, so a bundle of many lightly viewed channels might cost no more than a bundle of a few heavily viewed channels (a consistent cost per program).
- A degree of usage-related pricing (with discounts) would better track to value. That could limit the cord-cutting of light viewers, and obtain fair increases in revenue from heavy viewers (with price caps to ensure affordability).
- Customers could be alerted when they approach various budget thresholds, so they need not fear nasty surprises.

Again this can be done simply, without the advanced tracking and feedback processes of FairPay. Of course even greater tracking to value can be obtained with full use of the FairPay feedback process.

A similar use of post-bundling—*with* FairPay—was described in Chapter 10 for travel guides. That example also highlights the benefits of cross-supplier access (the Celestial Jukebox again)—with reasonable charging across suppliers managed through an aggregator. The old cable TV bundles at least gave us a single aggregated source for all our TV. Now that that is breaking down and moving toward a la carte, one can only hope that the TV industry will recognize the lose–lose inefficiency of separately priced walled gardens, and will find a better way to support aggregated access at reasonable prices (whether with FairPay or not).

CHAPTER 19

Producer/Creator Perspectives—Sustainable Value Propositions and Compensation Through the Supply Chain

If the idea of pricing for realized value makes sense at all, why not down through the supply chain? Some limited suggestions of how that might work have been discussed earlier. However, this gets into complex B2B relationships, and it is difficult to address this in very specific terms before there is more clarity on how businesses and consumers apply FairPay. So this chapter is a place-holder, merely intended to point in some general directions.

This discussion also applies to multisided markets, in which hub services enable an Actor-to-Actor market topology that can work as a supply chain. For example, a Web service may act as a marketplace linking consumers, advertisers, content providers, service providers, app developers, and the like (much as Facebook is currently seeking to do).

Some industries, such as journalism, have vertical integration and generally make use of in-house creative talent, so managing incentives and rewards in such supply chains is internal to the business, and thus relatively easy to manage. News providers can work out their own compensation structures with their journalists to exploit customer value feedback as a compensation factor, as discussed in Chapter 8. But, as noted there, even news often has independent supply sourcing and layers of curation and distribution—as is a current trend, as Facebook, Blendle, and others provide multisided markets for news.

Music makes for an interesting case study, since that industry already has all of the issues that make FairPay promising—and (as both good news and bad news) music has a well-developed supply chain with clear need for more fairness in pricing at all levels of the chain. Chapter 9 noted how this has become a high profile sore point, such as when the artist Taylor Swift pulled her music from Spotify, and then later got Apple to change the payment policy for their new music subscription service. Thus there is strong motivation to develop pricing that properly links the value proposition all the way up and down the chain, so that artists and fans, and those in between, are optimally aligned. These issues are briefly explored in that chapter.

Other industries have a range of supply chain models, some much like music, some with mixtures of in-house and independent creative supply, and some mostly in-house.

A core idea is that transparency can enhance the dialogs on value—and customer feedback on value should inform the sharing of the value surplus all along the chain. As we build out this Cloud of Value, customers should both have some transparency into how their payments are shared with creators and various layers of middlemen—and should have some say in those allocations. Similarly, the intermediate levels should partic- ipate in evaluation of what value they receive, and what they provide. This obviously needs to be done without undue complexity or friction, and with defaults that are workable when explicit guidance is lacking or impractical. It seems that there are many ways such structures could be developed, and just what shape they take is likely to depend on the nature of the business, the market, and the level of maturity in using FairPay. Early versions should keep it as simple as possible—but in time, some participation in pricing seems desirable and workable along all important levels of the chain.

PART IV

Toward a New Economics

CHAPTER 20

Why It Works—Behavioral Economics, Psychology, and Game Theory

More than Meets the Eye

FairPay draws on elements of pay what you want (PWYW) pricing—that simple strategy has gotten some attention in the past few years, but most people only dimly understand it. A growing body of research and actual usage is showing that it has much more potential value than most businesses realize. *People actually do pay even when they do not have to—often generously.*

For those who think there can be no real money in PWYW, the success of Humble Bundle shows that to be a misconception. They started with limited time offers of bundles of indie games, and later expanded to e-books. Their model includes a combination of payouts to developers and to charities. As of December 2014, it was reported that they had generated over $100M dollars for developers of games and other content sold in their bundles (since 2010), plus more than another $50M in additional customer revenues passed to charity. (In 2011, they raised $4.48M in funding from major venture capital firms.) One of the charities they support, the Electronic Frontier Foundation posted a nice summary (Kamdar 2011), observing that:

> While the record labels, movie studios, and video game producers have not figured out a way to compete with free, others have ... as the Humble Bundle has shown us, it is possible, with creators and distributors finding new and exciting ways to compete with free. ... when done right—developers, content providers, and even those who provide the business model can successfully compete with free.

There are many other real-world examples of PWYW successes in promotional sales—for both digital and real offerings—as summarized in the following sections (details and references at FPZLink).

Research on Making Customers Want to Pay You

Classical economics suggests that customers will pay zero if given a conventional PWYW offer (since payment is entirely voluntary). But recent business experiences and behavioral economics research suggest that thinking is just stuck in the mindset of the last century.

Modern mass-market commerce is a race to the bottom that assumes and appeals to the worst in people. Sellers set prices as high as they think they can to maximize total profit—so buyers' only option is to take it, or bargain-hunt. What we have here is what behavioral economists call an exchange relationship norm. Exchange norms are zero-sum, quid-pro-quo. Conventional PWYW changes that relationship in important ways—and FairPay does so far more deeply.

Insight into how and why real consumer pricing behavior is more generous than classical economics would have us think, emerges from a growing body of research and real business success with PWYW pricing. I summarize the key lessons in terms of a two-dimensional view of behavior that is my interpretation of a paper by Santana and Morwitz (2013), aptly titled "We're in This Together: How Sellers, Social Values, and Relationship Norms Influence Consumer Payments in Pay-What-You-Want Contexts":

1. Social Value Orientation (SVO), essentially pro-social versus proself—as *individual traits.*
2. Economic/Exchange Relationship Norms versus Communal Relationship Norms—as *situational variables* in a relationship.

This provides the motivation for the two-dimensional strategy that FairPay seeks to apply to getting buyers to willingly pay a fair price:

1. Segment customers based on their *Social Value Orientation traits*—are they receptive to and driven by social values, or not? Tactics for managing the FairPay process will be a bit different for high, medium, and low SVO segments.

2. Nudge all customers toward *Communal Relationship Norms*, in ways tuned to each segment—to seek to bring out their Social Value Orientation to the fullest extent possible.

Based on this, the FairPay process can be understood to work for each segment, but with rather different control parameters applied to each. In all cases the objective is to foster a situation that favors Communal Relationship Norms, and that draws out whatever level of Social Value Orientation can be elicited.

- The sweet spot is targeting high Social Value Orientation (pro-social) customers, and moving them toward Communal Relationship Norms. They are the ones who will respond best to the pricing privilege that the seller grants to the buyer in FairPay—to price in a way that considers fairness to the seller—and who will be least inclined to abuse that privilege. Managing that for these buyers will be mostly carrot, and not much stick.
- A secondary focus is on moving medium-to-low Social Value Orientation (more pro-self) customers toward Communal Relationship Norms. They will need more nudging to emphasize the carrot (why the seller is deserving of communal norms), while keeping the stick in sight (why it is in their best interest to price fairly). Those who do not respond with at least minimum levels of fairness (uncooperatively pro-self) can be treated as a third segment—to be excluded from Fair-Pay (at least until they seem ready to behave more sociably), and be left to buy on the conventional set-price terms that routinely work for pure Exchange Relationships.

Businesses can seek to maximize profits with a mix of FairPay and conventional set-pricing by doing the following (as explained throughout this book):

- Position themselves as deserving of Communal Relationship Norms. This can cover the whole spectrum of corporate citizenship, customer relations, quality, style, artistry, craftsmanship, service, and support.

- Sustain that positioning throughout their customer relationships. This is deeply embedded in the FairPay processes.
- Seek to market to high SVO (pro-social) customers as the preferred market segment. This is the segment that will be most willing to pay you generously for your product or service (if you position yourself as deserving, and ask in the right way).
- Manage the segmentation throughout the business processes to appeal in the right way to the right people. FairPay provides an architecture that supports this. In contrast, freemium has been very popular because of its simple segmentation between those who pay and those who don't, but has been limited in its ability to optimize and up-sell that, as explained earlier.

Such strategies for finding the sweet spots are especially important to targeting early uses of FairPay (as emphasized in Chapter 14). Given the learning curves and the risk that ill-targeted trials might lead to unsatisfying results, it is important that initial uses focus on customers who have high (pro-social) Social Value Orientations, in contexts in which they are appreciative and loyal, and so can be motivated to lean toward communal norms. That will favor the generosity and cooperation needed to make FairPay work well. Good results in such contexts will create a base for building out more broadly from there.

A further insight from this study is to reinforce that the nudging of buyers in the adaptive control process of FairPay is best done with a gentle hand. Communal Relationship Norms are a delicate thing. There is in FairPay an inherent quid-pro-quo over time (in the future, those who do not pay well will get fewer and less generous offers than those who do pay well). This should be managed with enough flexibility, generosity, and forgiveness of minor lapses, to reinforce, not poison, the effort to nudge toward Communal Relationship Norms. Much useful background is in the paper (as highlighted at FPZLink).

Making Pay What You Want Profitable and Sustainable

I summarized some specific points applicable to both simple PWYW, and the more sophisticated approach of FairPay when interviewed by Tom

Morkes, author of "*The Complete Guide to Pay What You Want Pricing*" (2013). That rich and useful guide is full of insights on best practices for making PWYW work that also apply to FairPay. PWYW draws on subtleties in human behavior—it can be very powerful, but there is nuance to framing such offers, and making it profitable on a sustained basis has been a challenge.

Tom provides a nice PWYW checklist. He lists 11 steps to making a PWYW offer work. I group Tom's list as follows, and add one more:

Numbers 1 to 4 are prerequisites to using these methods, both PWYW and FairPay:

1. Identify a competitive marketplace
2. Identify and target a demographic with fair-minded customers
3. Determine a product with low marginal cost
4. Create a product that can be sold credibly at a wide range of prices.

Numbers 5 to 11 enhance the process of using these methods, also relevant to PWYW and FairPay:

5. Establish a strong relationship with your customer
6. Clarify the offer
7. Show the customer that you're human (even large corporations can emphasize their human values and the people behind them)
8. Appeal to idealism
9. Anchor the price
10. Steer the customer to the right choice
11. Remind your audience to contribute.

To which FairPay adds a new 12th step, to roll it into a cyclic, adaptive, individualized process that is ongoing (a repeated game):

12. *Repeat offers contingent on fairness—build continuing relationship and dialog.*

Online Resource Guide to Pricing

I have posted a "Resource Guide to Pricing—Finding Fair Value Exchange" (Reisman 2016) as a partial survey of emerging research on PWYW and related pricing strategies. Some key points:

- A whole new era in pricing models is just beginning, spurred by the capabilities of the Internet. A nice summary of some of these directions is in the book *Smart Pricing* by Raju and Zhang of the Wharton School (Raju and Zhang 2010), which has illuminating chapters on PWYW and many other innovative models. Two other notable books on pricing are also listed (Anderson 2009; Nagle, Hogan, and Zale 2010).
- The Egbert, Greiff, and Xhangolli (2014) paper is particularly relevant to FairPay, as one of the few that highlights the value of post-pricing. This key element of FairPay has been under-recognized (when not missed completely) in most research and trials of PWYW.
- Others specific to PWYW are a series of research papers published since 2009—all the 12 included at this writing find it quite effective in a range of situations, revealing a number of reasons why people actually chose to pay, and to pay reasonably well, even when they do not have to. One (Gneezy et al. 2010) also looks at PWYW combined with a share of proceeds to charity, which was found to be particularly effective (more in Chapter 22). Another (Regner and Barria 2009) focuses on a very interesting online indie music distributor with a PWYW model (combining a try-before-you-buy feature and a high revenue share with artists, both seen as enhancing payment levels). Natter and Kaufmann (2015) is one of the most comprehensive recent surveys of this body of work.

While many of these papers are written for academics, business people would do well to give them a look (skipping over the heavy parts, and with just reasonable caution that some of these models and experiments are simplified). Also, the Wikipedia article on PWYW is regularly updated and has useful information, including links to information on notable real uses of PWYW. In addition, I am collaborating on a paper with Adrian Payne and Pennie Frow that is to include an extensive survey of PWYW from the perspective of dynamically participative co-pricing strategies such as FairPay (to be cited at FPZLink when available).

Broad Grounding in Behavioral Economics

Nobel Prize winning economist Daniel Kahneman's book, *Thinking Fast and Slow* (2011) presents a wide range of insights into how we think and make choices. These insights—mostly established in the past few decades, and only beginning to be widely recognized—form the groundwork for the new field of behavioral economics. Kahneman's book shows how greatly people are influenced by framing and anchors. While our decision processes are wonderfully rich and nuanced, they are highly susceptible to influence. Much of our decision making is based on the fast, intuitive, but error-prone processes Kahneman calls System 1—with reluctant intervention by the slower, more deliberative and "rational" processes of System 2, which is often lazy, and also subject to systematic errors.

As we have seen, FairPay introduces a model in which the buyer chooses the price, but with incentives to consider whether the seller will judge it to be fair, in that particular context. Counterbalancing that, the seller has the ultimate power to motivate fair pricing by controlling whether future FairPay offers will be made to that buyer. The seller can also *frame* the offer, and set a *suggested price* as an *anchor*. Applying the principles of behavioral economics as outlined by Kahneman, the seller has many opportunities to *nudge* buyers to price fairly and even generously. Many of these lessons are very relevant to FairPay:

- *Framing* is very powerful and applies to both System 1 and System 2. Choices can be altered very dramatically by framing the choice in different ways. The core objective is to make buyers feel that the seller deserves a fair price, and to find incentives for pricing generously.
- *Nudge* (Thaler and Sunstein 2009) is the title of another book (based on work also described by Kahneman) that makes much of *choice architectures* that can nudge behavior in very powerful ways. A choice architecture is a systematic process for framing choices to induce desired behaviors. FairPay sellers can use such choice architectures to nudge most buyers to set prices to desirable levels.
- *Anchors* are an aspect of framing, providing a reference point for a price or other parameter to be chosen. Even where the

individual is free to ignore the anchor entirely, it tends to have a surprisingly strong influence on their choice. Fair-Pay exploits the power of suggested prices as psychological anchors to nudge buyer pricing choices.

- *Intensity matching* is one of the things the intuitive and automatic System 1 does easily. Matching prices to one's happiness with a product is easy. Thus choosing prices that match to perceived value is also easy (see the next section on tipping), and the desire to pay fairly for being delighted by a seller can be harnessed just as well, and perhaps better, than the competing desire to find bargains.
- *WYSIATI* (What You See Is All There Is)—people (especially their System 1), tend to make choices based on just the factors they see, and even System 2 is lazy and tends not to search for other factors that may be missing. A key objective of framing and choice architecture is to present those factors that cause buyers to notice what they should value (and to downplay any negatives) in order to nudge toward desirable pricing choices.
- The laziness of System 2 is perhaps most strikingly evident in the use of opt-in versus opt-out choices to set desirable defaults. Thus making acceptance of a suggested price an opt-out choice (such as for ongoing subscriptions) might lead most buyers to be compliant, most of the time (especially once a comfort level is established).
- Decisions are affected by distortions in psychological weighting.
  - o Loss aversion is stronger than gain-seeking. Losses from an established position tend to be weighted more heavily than equivalent gains. Once a buyer has the privilege of setting prices under FairPay, they will be averse to losing that privilege (by pricing unfairly low just to get a small gain on one transaction).
  - o Fear of disappointment also tends to be overweighted. The post-experience pricing of FairPay eliminates the risk of buyer remorse, and that fear can be a significant barrier to buyers accepting a price corresponding to full value up-front. Pre-set prices are implicitly discounted in the

buyer's mind to allow for that risk. FairPay removes that discount factor.

- Perceptions of fairness and entitlement are inherently frame-specific and not underlying. By framing fair prices as being context-dependent—such as based on usage, value obtained, ability to pay, and other factors—buyers can be nudged to accept prices that are different from those for other buyers in different circumstances. Those who pay a higher price will not feel regret on learning that another paid less, if they are helped to see that the equity of the price depends on the circumstances (different entitlements in different contexts).

Building on how System 1 and System 2 partner in making choices, an objective of FairPay choice architecture is to make it easy for the buyer to accept seller-suggested prices so that both buyer and seller maintain a happy and mutually valuable commercial relationship.

Kahneman mentions *cognitive ease* as a key factor in how we make choices. When things are going well, with no surprises or threats, System 1 does its automatic control—but when there is cognitive strain, System 2 reluctantly jumps in. Obviously, FairPay pricing processes should seek to maximize cognitive ease, as they nudge buyers to fair pricing.

- The *causes of cognitive ease* are:
  - Repeated experience: As buyers become familiar with Fair-Pay, and with a given seller, they will gain comfort and ease.
  - Clear display: Offers and pricing requests should frame the offer and the suggested price as simply and clearly as possible.
  - Primed idea: Offers and pricing requests should frame the value proposition, the relevant context, and the suggested price to most effectively prime the buyer to accept it as fair.
  - Good mood: FairPay aligns the motives of the seller and the buyer—if the seller delights the buyer and positions himself as a positive and deserving partner and provider of value, the buyer will find it easy to reward that (just as most people give good tips to delightful and effective waiters, and pay premiums to companies that delight them—such as Apple).

- The *consequences of cognitive ease* are: Feelings of familiarity, truth, goodness, and effortlessness.

All of this suggests that effective choice architectures can be applied to make FairPay very effective for most buyers—*if* the seller really seeks to deliver what the buyer values, in return for a fair profit for doing that.

Some aspects of choice architecture and nudging may smack of exploitation of buyers by manipulative businesses—but remember, this is in the context of a system in which *buyers have complete power to set any price they think fair*. The choice architecture is just a *defensive* tool for sellers to nudge buyers toward fairness in choices they have full freedom to make. The nudging of a choice architecture may be "manipulative" to a degree, but in the context of an unprecedented level of buyer freedom—sellers need some compensatory powers (and it seems that abuse is unlikely and easily countered).

Cognitive Ease and Lessons from Tipping

Further insight into the cognitive ease of FairPay can be seen from some parallels with restaurant tipping (more at FPZLink). Some people dislike tipping (especially outside the United States) but it has strong appeals. It gives patrons the right to match tips to the value of the service, rewarding good service (sometimes very generously) and pricing lower for poor service. It is widely recognized that when restaurant service is built into prices, with no discretionary reward for service quality, service is often poor and customers dissatisfied. There are of course some customers who tip unfairly. But the problem decreases among regular customers, and it is in just such long-term relationship contexts that FairPay seems most likely to do well (and use of FairPay can be limited to such contexts).

Tipping teaches us how easy it is for people to compute value intuitively. On hearing about FairPay, people often ask "isn't it a cognitive burden for customers to have to think about the value?" But tipping shows that this kind of evaluation is not difficult—it is highly intuitive. We easily do a complex multivariate, multidimensional analysis in our head, during and after a meal, and know immediately whether we think the service was average, better, or worse, and by roughly what degree

(Kahneman's intensity matching). We can then easily figure whether to adjust our average tipping level up or down, plus whether to adjust for being a regular or any other special factors, to determine that we should tip X percent. (The only difficulty is just doing the arithmetic of how much X percent is—and that is easily automated away.)

So the behavioral economics of tipping is very supportive of the idea that FairPay will prove very effective in selected business contexts.

FairPay as a Repeated Game

Game theory offers very compelling support for *FairPay as a repeated game*, and perhaps can serve as a powerful tool to help design FairPay journeys that will push this game toward highly win–win behaviors. As noted earlier, the problem with most current pricing methods is that they are transaction-focused, as one-time games, and not relationship-focused, as repeated games. Structuring the customer relationship as a repeated game promises to add strong incentives to build a reputation for paying fairly—even at a short-term cost—in order to get a continuing stream of attractive offers in the future.

This seems a compelling argument that FairPay can be made to work very effectively once both sides understand the game. I have only limited understanding of game theory, but a paper on "The Evolution of Cooperation in Infinitely Repeated Games" (Bó and Fréchette 2011) seems to support that. The paper explains that there are a number of issues that affect the level of cooperation that is actually achieved, and that may not correspond to theoretical equilibrium, but "cooperation does prevail … when the probability of continuation and the payoff from cooperation are high enough." That seems to reinforce my expectation that FairPay will generally work if the business makes the repeated game attractive to the customer, and applies reasonable (but not unduly harsh) controls on FairPay credit outstanding to limit the losses in cases where the customer fails to cooperate.

CHAPTER 21

New Dimensions of Value— Customer Contributions

The focus of FairPay on value exchange as perceived and considered fair and equitable by both the customer and the provider, enable it to encompass much broader aspects of value than are conventionally reflected in prices. An important aspect of that is the customer's contribution to the co-creation of value, including value delivered in reverse, to the supplier, as captured by the idea of a "reverse meter." We have seen that most clearly in journalism (Chapter 8), but also in music and other businesses. Major aspects of value include:

From the provider to the customer, FairPay focuses on the total value of all kinds, as actually delivered to each particular customer—the value-in-use, in-context, for exactly what is consumed and how (what items, how many, how intensely), including the core product/service, plus membership perks, and so on—the value of that experience and potentially even the outcomes that result (use, enjoyment, appreciation, and even the value of results/outcomes enabled). This can also include "soft" values, such as

- Service and support;
- Participation, listening, and responsiveness (access to creators before or after creation);
- Related products and services; and
- The social value of production and production processes, community services, and good corporate citizenship.

From the customer to the provider, FairPay considers not just monetary payments (subscription or membership fees, or pay-per-use), but other currencies. Thus it factors in credits (the "reverse meter") for:

- Attention to advertising (including the possibility of custom-ized levels of ad loads);
- Personal data that can be used or sold (again with possible customization);
- The value of user-generated content;
- The value of viral promotion and leads; and
- Volunteer-provided services to the provider.

Many of these reverse value elements can be significant for some customers in many businesses. Even when considered in the most rudi-mentary way, this holistic view of value should feed back into the fairness reputation of each customer—a customer who has valid claims of provid-ing value to the business should reasonably be given some credit for that in assessing the fairness of their direct payments.

Perhaps the most common customer value contribution in many businesses is advertising (to the point that many do not charge directly at all). As we have seen, there is growing dissatisfaction on both sides with digital advertising. There is urgent need to find a new form of win–win value exchange that extracts the most value from advertising that is acceptable and effective with a given customer, while avoiding forms that are not, and adapting to varying perceptions about that.

CHAPTER 22

Societal Perspectives—Markets That Center on Human Values

Turning the Invisible Hand to Create Shared Value

"Creating Shared Value" (Kramer and Porter 2011), the influential 2011 HBR article by Porter and Kramer, suggests the need to reinvent capitalism with broader ideas about value creation that will unleash a wave of innovation and growth. FairPay speaks to that need. They propose that "creating shared value represents a broader conception of Adam Smith's invisible hand." They nicely draw the big picture for shared value, noting that, unlike calls for "Corporate Social Responsibility" that are at odds with profit motivations:

> Shared value focuses companies on the right kind of profits—profits that create societal benefits rather than diminish them. ...

> The moment for an expanded view of value creation has come. A host of factors, such as the growing social awareness of employees and citizens and the increased scarcity of natural resources, will drive unprecedented opportunities to create shared value.

> We need a more sophisticated form of capitalism, one imbued with a social purpose. But that purpose should arise not out of charity but out of a deeper understanding of competition and economic value creation.

They suggest what we need is not "a redistribution approach," but one for "expanding the total pool of economic and social value."

We have seen how FairPay creates a new market regime that reorients the invisible hand toward shared value (an invisible handshake), one that can be operationalized in business today, to offer an entirely new microeconomics for profit-seeking business transactions. FairPay takes this Creating Shared Value (CSV) big picture and provides *methods for "doing business as business,"* which support that vision. These methods can be applied now, in a wide range of businesses, and will point the way to applying similar new thinking more generally.

As we saw, Adam Smith's invisible hand works at a transaction level: it optimizes the balance of supply and demand in terms of prices for large numbers of individual transactions. The invisible hand does not know or care about repeat business or shared value (except as it affects demand in aggregate). It ignores sustainability and other aspects of social value ("externalities"). It is this blindness to past and future relationships that creates many of the problems in conventional market economics. There is no direct way to factor in long-term consequences for the individual parties, or society as a whole. Addressing those "externalities" by bolting on special measures (taxes, subsidies, etc.) is artificial and very problematic.

FairPay turns the invisible hand into an invisible handshake, working over time, at the relationship level: *it optimizes the balance of supply and demand, in terms of prices over time, with respect to individual customers and what they value.* Relationship pricing is balanced through an ongoing series of pricing conversations, to achieve an agreed-upon level of shared value in each of a multitude of ongoing buyer–seller relationships. This creates prices that reflect not just financial value, but whatever dimensions of human or social value the producer–customer pair want to reflect in the dialogs about value. There is no need for added bottom lines, or separate CSV objectives—CSV is integral to the handshake. Sustainability can factor in directly (and cross-market factors still apply, but are secondary).

The essence of FairPay is that buyers and sellers engage in a continuing individualized dialog about shared value—both at a personal and a social level—as actually realized in every transaction.

- *FairPay seeks maximum shared value for each customer, by being specific to the value sought and received by that customer, at that time, in that context.* It reflects individual variations in need, value perception, willingness to pay, ability to pay, and all relevant criteria. It provides sellers with fine-grained, in-context "market""data for segments of one, that enable the sellers to fully understand market needs, and learn new ways to meet them, and to delight their customers, one by one.

- *It naturally reflects broad considerations of shared social value beyond the individual customer, by sharing responsibility with the customer for the social valuation process.* Buyers are free to consider whether a seller is socially responsible in the larger sense, and to factor that into their willingness to pay (to whatever extent they desire). What might have been an externality to the seller may be internalized by the buyer, so that the seller must internalize it as well. Social values shift from external constraints at odds with profit maximization to natural subjects of the value dialog with the buyer. Whatever values the customer thinks are important are reflected in this balance.
- *It changes the equation from a zero-sum game of buyers shopping around for the lowest prices and sellers seeking to be the low-cost provider, to a win–win collaboration for achieving shared value.*
- *Instead of consumers seeing profits as coming at their expense, profits are framed as a valid and deserved sharing of their value surplus with a company that is a respected partner in value creation.* This gives a new legitimacy to profit-seeking, as integral to collaborative creation of shared value.

Traditional transaction-level pricing models foster a purely price-based race to the bottom, which makes it hard for a company to see at a microeconomic level how social responsibility to their customers and the larger public can benefit their bottom line—well intentioned as they may be. We can talk of shifting the view to long-term profit maximization, but how do we do that? The ongoing, relationship-based structure of FairPay microeconomics directly considers shared value, at both the individual and larger level, in a way that removes the conflict. It aligns profit maximization for the firm with maximization of social value (at least to the extent that is perceived by individual buyers). *Thus FairPay provides a new microeconomic mechanism to seek long-term profit maximization in ways that directly align with social value maximization.*

FairPay naturally guides better economic efficiency, while significantly reflecting the broader context of shared human value. By giving consumers a say in pricing, human and social values can be served as just another business opportunity to provide service for profit, not a "Corporate Social Responsibility" cost. FairPay provides a structure for pricing that is dependent on buyer acceptance in a way that legitimizes differential pricing—to efficiently address varying value perceptions, usage patterns, abilities to pay—and social values. Price "discrimination" becomes an equitable method for maximizing shared value when the buyer participates in the discrimination and accepts the rationale for what they pay, and whether it is more or less than other buyers.

This buyer acceptance of "fair and reasonable price discrimination" also enables new ways to efficiently address low-income and disadvantaged markets at a profit (and social benefit). For example, it becomes clear that those who can afford to pay more than others should do so. Information and digital services that may be expensive in high-value/high-ability-to-pay markets can fairly be offered far more cheaply in disadvantaged markets without cannibalizing the markets where buyers know they can and should fairly share their large value surplus. When treated as partners in shared value pricing decisions, consumers will recognize that companies should be able to profit more (and recover more of their costs) from those who can afford it than from those who cannot, and companies will be able to expand and differentiate their markets accordingly.

How Consumers Can Nudge Corporations for Good

Richard Thaler raised some interesting points in an op-ed (Thaler 2015) about "The Power of Nudges, for Good and Bad." "Nudges, small design changes that can markedly affect individual behavior, have been catching on" he observes, and then explains his concern that: "Many companies are nudging purely for their own profit and not in customers' best interests." He concludes the piece with this observation (emphasis added):

> As customers, we can help one another by resisting these come-ons. The more we turn down questionable offers like trip insurance and scrutinize "one month" trials, the less incentive companies

will have to use such schemes. Conversely, *if customers reward firms that act in our best interests, more such outfits will survive and flourish, and the options available to us will improve.*

I take that as a nice statement of the power of FairPay to directly reward firms that work with us to serve our joint best interests.

- Using FairPay, firms and consumers can jointly create a virtuous cycle in which the consumer nudges the firm to understand what they value and are willing to pay for, and the firm rewards those consumers who work with them by delivering more of what those consumers show that they value.
- This builds customer journeys around cycles architected to build a mutually beneficial relationship of service, value, profit, and loyalty.

From this perspective, the appeal of FairPay is in how it deepens the relationship between a firm and its customers to be more open and responsive, and shifts focus toward value—in context, in the broadest sense, over the life of the relationship:

- It not only channels the nudges from the company to the customer, but also creates a framework for nudges from the customer to the company.
- Customers who use FairPay fairly will get the most value, and companies who use FairPay effectively will attract and keep the most profitable and loyal customers.

Value Is the Single Bottom Line

Because the conventional bottom line ignores many socially important aspects of shared social value, companies have tried to tack on a second or third or fourth bottom line to reflect values of "people" and "planet" in addition to "profit." The problem is that these are just tacked on to organizations that have evolved to maximize profit, and getting them to consistently pay more than lip service to other kinds of value is very difficult. Further measures include new kinds of social enterprise entities that formally recognize the importance of social values, including benefit corporations (B-Corps) that are clearly relieved of legal obligation to maximize profit. But still, an artifice.

With FairPay, consumers can push businesses to accept their judgements of value as including human or social values, to the extent the consumer wants and the business accepts as reasonable. When that happens, it goes directly into the single bottom line. There is no need for other bottom lines. That also means that a company's revenue is a real metric of its value contribution. When we roll revenue into a Gross National Product (GNP), we automatically include all of the value that such revenue reflects. Value-in-context in the micro rolls directly into value in the macro.

Of course there may be forms of value, such as externalities that consumers do not choose to reflect into their dialogs on value, and thus their pricing. So one might wonder if we need a special bottom line for those. But if they are known and legitimate, wouldn't it be more effective to just introduce them into the core dialog about value, reach whatever level of agreement is possible, and have prices reflect them accordingly?

FairPay as a Step Toward "Freedom To ..."

Tom Friedman (2011) pointed to the emergence of a new level of democracy in many domains, in which consumers are gaining more equal power with organizations of all kinds. We are only at the beginning stages of this (as Friedman quotes Dov Seidman):

> when people are creating a lot of "freedom from" things—freedom from oppression or whatever system is in their way—but have not yet scaled the values and built the institutional frameworks that enable "freedom to"—freedom to build a career, a business or a meaningful life.

Friedman observes that we need leadership to find the "to."

FairPay is an institutional framework for one "freedom to" that can change the world of commerce for the better—the freedom to set our prices, constrained only by a responsibility to be fair about it. The institutional framework is an architecture for dialogs with customers that enable that freedom. It works by linking that consumer freedom to set prices to complementary methods that give sellers the freedom to manage the pricing risk related to that new customer freedom.

Doing Well by Doing Good—Shared Social Responsibility and Pricing

A perspective on the psychology of how social responsibility can factor into FairPay pricing process is apparent from recent experience with pay what you want (PWYW) pricing. There is clear evidence that adding charitable giving to the pricing process can significantly increase total revenue and profit. This was the finding of the Gneezy et al. (2010) paper mentioned earlier. The finding was for charity combined with PWYW, but the lesson seems equally applicable to charity combined with FairPay.

As reported, PWYW+charity yielded significantly higher total profit than PWYW, alone, without charity, and also more than either a simple set-price, or set-price+charity.

- Individually, the PWYW buyers paid less than the set-price buyers, but far more of them made a purchase. In this case the product was a photo of the participant taken during an amusement park ride. Purchase rates were very low with standard pricing (at $12.95) and only slightly higher when 50 percent of that price went to charity.
- As summarized in the Discover blog:

… But when customers could pay what they wanted in the knowledge that half of that would go to charity, sales *and* profits went through the roof. Around 4.5% of the customers asked for a photo (up 9 times from the standard price plan), and on average, each one paid $5.33 for the privilege. Even after taking away the charitable donations, that still left Gneezy with a decent profit. … This is a substantial result, especially since it came from a real setting. The theme park that Gneezy used stands to make another $600,000 a year in profits if it takes up her sales strategy. And just to be sure, Gneezy confirmed that sales at a nearby souvenir shop didn't fall on the days when she ran her study. These extra profits weren't coming at a cost to retailers elsewhere in the park.

These results suggest that combining FairPay with charity could have even better results, possibly even with much lower levels of charity, and thus higher profit. The charity component encourages people to buy, and to pay a fair price, and the FairPay feedback process provides even more incentive to pay a fair price. FairPay *without* charity can also prove effective, and be more widely applicable—by focusing similar motivations of generosity and altruism toward deserving businesses—but the combination certainly seems worth trying. Gneezy describes this use of charity as "shared social responsibility," a variation on "corporate social responsibility," which gets to issues of how corporations seek to build a more collaborative relationship with customers. FairPay is a complementary way to build more collaborative relationships, and to do so more directly and efficiently. Whether the combination is more or less effective than FairPay alone, remains to be seen, and probably depends on the details of the situation.

These results also show how much profit, and how much of the addressable market, can be lost under conventional pricing. Sixteen times more people bought photos when given the ability to pay what they wanted (but they paid poorly), so that suggests an opportunity, but is still problematic. But nine times more people bought with PWYW+charity—and they paid at a rate that tripled profits! Perhaps inspired by this study, a notable business has been built on a similar combination of PWYW with charity—Humble Bundle (as discussed in Chapter 20) and others such as PledgeMusic have done so as well.

CHAPTER 23

Competing on Vendor Lifetime Value

Competition is a central driver of our market economics, and FairPay can lead to a new logic for competition. FairPay can be a powerful tool for firms to create stronger loyalty loops that significantly raise barriers to competition—but it also empowers new kinds of competition on fairness.

Most of this book focuses on the ability of FairPay to expand markets and grow total value—seeking optimal on average and in total, even if not on every transaction—from the perspective of the firm-customer dyad. But what about the larger market ecosystem—competition among firms and the innovation and efficiency that creates? The barrier to new/better entrants and possible loss of innovation and efficiency is an issue to think about. Consider the example of Amazon, with its winner-take-most scale economies, and its use of Prime loyalty services—and how that power might increase further if FairPay were added in. How can other firms compete?—and does that matter?

At one level, the greater customer feedback/response arising out of the reliably cooperative relationship compensates in many respects for some reduction of direct competition. As a consumer, I like the convenience and reliability of Amazon Prime, caring less about occasionally missing slightly better deals. But we need enough competition to keep the winner on track. As long as there is fringe of competition—bargain suppliers on the low end and boutiques at the high end—perhaps that will be enough. And as an alternative, there could be a large competing cross-merchant FairPay platform that serves any and all Amazon competitors with a consolidated fairness reputation database, as described in Chapter 13.

Also, tools to help customers compare vendors based on vendor fairness (how responsive, understanding, and reasonable a business is in managing its FairPay processes) can be expected to emerge, so the customers can keep tabs on *how vendors compete on fairness.*

But looking more broadly, perhaps this is just another aspect of the shift from Goods-Dominant Logic notions of competition on the production and sale of goods, to Service-Dominant Logic notions of *competition on collaborative co-creation of services.* Lusch and Vargo (2014) speak of "a collaborative advantage that can lead to competitive advantage and improved system viability." They detail "five major sources of collaborative advantage: collaborative process competency, absorptive competency, adaptive competency, resource integration competency, and learning competency." FairPay is more or less directly aimed at enhancing all of these competencies. So perhaps it may not drive to lowest costs, but it seems to drive toward most effective value co-creation.

Just as companies are increasingly seeking to maximize Customer Lifetime Value, shouldn't customers seek to maximize Vendor Lifetime Value? Won't the dialogs about value keep the focus on jointly learning about, absorbing, and adapting to any innovations and efficiencies that customers discover in the market, as long as some reasonable level of competition exists?

(And, of course, *FairPay customers compete on fairness as well.* A central tenet of FairPay is that the more fair customers are to their vendors, the more and better offers they get.)

CHAPTER 24

Taking Action— Implementation of FairPay

As noted at the outset, this book is a call to action—to get people to see the potential, and help move FairPay into practice.

I believe the case is compelling that FairPay can not only solve serious and urgent problems of making businesses sustainably profitable, but can also lead us toward a new economic nirvana—a way to build adaptively win–win relationships that are much better for business, consumers, and society as a whole:

- A workable balance of powers that lets consumers have far more say in things, and makes it desirable and sustainable for producers to co-create value with them on that basis.
- A new social contract in the form of an invisible handshake that guides allocation of a "share of wallet" to fairly sustain creators, and the services that support them and distribute their work, to create the greatest value possible.

All the key strategies are empirically well supported as effective individually, and there is good reason to expect that they will work together roughly as described here (after an initial shakedown and tuning process)—as a self-sustaining, repeated game. (Do check FPZLink for updates on field trials—and let me know of trials that should be reported.)

Learn, Adjust, Pivot

The next step is to engage in trials, learn from them, and build on them—focusing on subsets of customers most likely to be receptive early adopters. Even if some of the details are wrong, and some of the human element is harder to wrangle than expected, it seems clear that the direction is sound.

We should be able to learn from any initial disappointments and figure out how to do better. That could be very rapid, but maybe it will be in fits and starts, and perhaps this process will take some surprising turns. But in any case, such experimentation promises to drive us to a new logic that proves workable and increasingly effective. And in the meantime, it can serve as a productive thought experiment.

Spread the Word

You can help get these ideas to those who can spread them and build on them. It is natural to have some concerns about such a radical paradigm shift— but those who recognize how deep this runs can help get others to see. (Guide them to FairPayZone.com)

I am working on FairPay on a pro-bono basis. My primary objective is to get these ideas out there, find opportunities to do proof of concept testing and refinement of the strategy, and to foster its wide adoption.

Additional Information and Updates Are Online—Feedback Invited

This book draws heavily from my FairPayZone.com blog, which remains the home for my continuing work on FairPay. Supplementary information on FairPay, the story so far, and updates on ongoing development can be found there. A special landing page for readers of this book is at *FPZlink.com*. I plan to include a forum there for open discussion and development of a community of interest. I can be reached through that site, and welcome dialog with readers.

Online Supplement—FPZLink—at FPZLink.com

An online supplement to this book provides more background and examples, links to references, as well as updates.

The FairPay Manifesto

- Markets want to be smart and finely adapted to incentives.
- The Internet wants to be smart and adaptive.
- The Internet enables direct feedback that is immensely rich and timely.
- Direct feedback is the most powerful way to tune incentives.
- Free is inherently dumb, because it obscures market incentives.
- Set prices do not reflect value-as-realized (by individual buyers).
- Prices should correspond to value-as-realized.
- Buyers, not sellers, perceive value-as-realized.
- Sellers should measure and manage buyer perception of value-as-realized.
- Maximize buyer perception of value-as-realized and a fair price will follow.
- A good pricing process is a conversation.
- The way to do pricing is to be a pricing process.

(As originally published online, June 20, 2010 (Reisman 2010). With homage to The Cluetrain Manifesto … and Lao-Tzu.)

References

(*A version of this listing with live hyperlinks is available at FPZLink.*)

Anderson, C. 2006a. *The Long Tail: Why the Future of Business Is Selling Less of More.* New York: Hyperion.

Anderson, C. 2006b. "About Me" (The Long Tail Chris Anderson's blog). www.longtail.com/about.html

Anderson, C. 2009. *Free: How Today's Smartest Businesses Profit by Giving Something for Nothing.* New York: Hachette Books.

Bertini, M., and O. Koenigsberg. 2014. "When Customers Help Set Prices." *MIT Sloan Management Review* 55, no. 4, p. 57.

Bertini, M., and R. Reisman. November 18, 2013. "When Selling Digital Content, Let the Customer Set the Price." *Harvard Business Review Blog.* https://hbr.org/2013/11/when-selling-digital-content-let-the-customer-set-the-price/

Bezos, J. 2013. "Jeff Bezos on Post Purchase." *The Washington Post*, August 5.

Blossom, J. November 7, 2011. "Pay as You Exit: FairPay Explores New Content Pricing Discovery Regimes." *ContentBlogger.* http://contentblogger.shorecominc.com/2011/11/pay-as-you-exit-fairpay-explores-new.html

Bó, P.D., and G.R. Fréchette. 2011. "The Evolution of Cooperation in Infinitely Repeated Games: Experimental Evidence." *The American Economic Review* 101, no. 1, pp. 411–29.

Bosworth, A. September 16, 2015. "Salesforce IoT Cloud: Connecting the Internet of Things to Your Customers." *Salesforce Blog.* www.salesforce.com/blog/2015/09/introducing-iot-cloud-thunder.html

Carr, D. 2010. "Dialing in a Plan: The Times Installs a Meter on Its Future." *The New York Times*, January 20.

Carr, D. 2013. "An Interview with Pierre Omidyar." *The New York Times*, October 20.

Carvell, A. July 6, 2010. "Greater Proportion of Free Apps on Android than iPhone." www.geek.com/apple/greater-proportion-of-free-apps-on-android-than-iphone-1268052/

Cox, B.J. 1996. *Superdistribution: Objects as Property on the Electronic Frontier.* 1st ed. New York: Addison-Wesley.

Edelman, D.C., and M. Singer. November 2015. "Competing on Customer Journeys." *Harvard Business Review.*

Egbert, H., M. Greiff, and K. Xhangolli. 2014. "PWYW Pricing ex post Consumption: A Sales Strategy for Experience Goods." Munich Personal RePEc Archive. https://mpra.ub.uni-muenchen.de/53376/

Elmer-DeWitt, P. 2010. "App Store: 1% of Apple's Gross Profit." *Fortune*, June 23.

Farhi, P. 2013. "Jeffrey Bezos, Washington Post's Next Owner, Aims for a New 'Golden Era' at the Newspaper" [interview]. *The Washington Post*, September 2.

Friedman, T. 2011. "Help Wanted." *New York Times*, December 18.

Frow, P., R. Reisman, and A. Payne. June 11, 2015. "Co-Pricing: Co-Creating Customer Value Through Dynamic Value Propositions." *SSRN*. http://ssrn.com/abstract=2634197

Gneezy, A., U. Gneezy, L. Nelson, and A. Brown. July 16, 2010. "Shared Social Responsibility: A Field Experiment in Pay-What-You-Want Pricing and Charitable Giving." *Science* 329, no. 5989, pp. 325–27.

Greig, A. March 2016. "Winning Back Lost Customers." *Harvard Business Review*.

Ha, A. May 7, 2013. "BitTorrent Steps Up Monetization Efforts By Taking Its (Potentially Paywalled) Content Bundles into Alpha." TechCrunch. https://techcrunch.com/2013/05/07/bittorrent-bundle/

Hayek, F.A. 1944. *The Road to Serfdom*. Chicago, IL: University of Chicago Press.

Henry, J. 2013. "Why I Bought the Globe." *Boston Globe*, October 27.

Hufford, A. 2015. "U.S. Stocks Drop on Media Meltdown: Fears of 'Cord-Cutting' by Consumers Jolt Stocks of Traditional Media Firms." *The Wall Street Journal*, August 6.

Iansiti, M., and K.R. Lakhani. 2014. "Digital Ubiquity: How Connections, Sensors, and Data Are Revolutionizing Business (Digest Summary)." *Harvard Business Review* 92, no. 11, pp. 91–99.

IFPI. April 12, 2016. IFPI Global Music Report 2016. www.ifpi.org/news/IFPI-GLOBAL-MUSIC-REPORT-2016

Jarvis, J. December 19, 2011. "Why not a Reverse Meter?" BuzzMachine. http://buzzmachine.com/2011/12/19/why-not-a-reverse-meter/

Kahneman, D. 2011. *Thinking, Fast and Slow*. Macmillan.

Kaiser, R.G. October 16, 2014. *The Bad News About the News*. MA: The Brookings Essay. www.brookings.edu/research/essays/2014/bad-news#

Kamdar, A. August 8, 2011. "Developers and Fans Benefit from Humble Indie Bundle Pay-What-You-Want Model." Electronic Frontier Foundation (EFF). www.eff.org/deeplinks/2011/08/developers-and-fans-benefit-humble-indie-bundle

Kramer, M.R., and M.E. Porter. 2011. "Creating Shared Value." *Harvard Business Review* 89, nos. 1/2, pp. 62–77.

Kumar, V. May 2014. "Making 'Freemium' Work." *Harvard Business Review*.

Levine, R. 2011. *Free Ride: How Digital Parasites Are Destroying the Culture Business, and How the Culture Business Can Fight Back*. New York: Random House.

Lusch, R.F., and S.L. Vargo. 2014. *Service-Dominant Logic: Premises, Perspectives, Possibilities*. Cambridge: Cambridge University Press.

McKinney, K. February 6, 2015. "This Horribly Dull Government Report Could Change Music Forever. We Read It for You." Vox Technology. www.vox.com/2015/2/6/7992391/copyright-office-music-report

Morkes, T. 2013. *The Complete Guide to Pay What You Want Pricing*. http://tommorkes.com/pwywguide/

Nagle, T., J. Hogan, and J. Zale. 2010. *The Strategy and Tactics of Pricing*. New York: Prentice Hall.

Natter, M., and K. Kaufmann. 2015. "Voluntary Market Payments: Underlying Motives, Success Drivers and Success Potentials." *Journal of Behavioral and Experimental Economics* 57, pp. 149–57.

Omidyar, P. 2013. "My Next Adventure in Journalism" First posted at www.omidyargroup.com/pov/2013/10/16/my-next-adventure-in-journalism/ Republished at www.huffingtonpost.com/pierre-omidyar/my-next-adventure-in-jour_b_4114672.html

Osterwalder, A., and Y. Pigneur. 2010. *Business Model Generation: A Handbook for Visionaries, Game Changers, and Challengers*. Hoboken, NJ: John Wiley & Sons.

Osterwalder, A., Y. Pigneur, G. Bernarda, and A. Smith. 2014. *Value Proposition Design: How to Create Products and Services Customers Want* (Strategyzer). Hoboken, NJ: John Wiley & Sons.

PageFair. 2015. "The 2015 Ad Blocking Report." https://pagefair.com/blog/2015/ad-blocking-report/

Pareles, J. 2007. "Pay What You Want for This Article." *The New York Times*, December 9.

Payne, A., and P. Frow. 2013. *Strategic Customer Management*. Cambridge: Cambridge University Press.

Peoples, G. 2013. "Amanda Palmer Q&A: Why Pay-What-You-Want Is the Way Forward, and More." *Billboard*, January 28.

Piano. August 11, 2015. Piano Media and Tinypass Merge. Business Wire. www.businesswire.com/news/home/20150811005722/en/Piano-Media-Tinypass-Merge

Raju, J., and Z.J. Zhang. 2010. *Smart Pricing: How Google, Priceline, and Leading Businesses Use Pricing Innovation for Profitability*. Upper Saddle River, NJ: Wharton School Publishing.

Regner, T., and J. Barria. 2009. "Do Consumers Pay Voluntarily? The Case of Online Music." *Journal of Economic Behavior & Organization* 71, no. 2, pp. 395–406.

Reisman, R. June 20, 2010. "FairPay: The Future of a Radical Pricing Process." The FairPay Zone. www.fairpayzone.com/p/fairpay-future-of-radical-pricing.html

Reisman, R., and M. Bertini. November 26, 2014. "A Novel Architecture to Monetize Digital Goods." *SSRN.* http://ssrn.com/abstract=2530347

Reisman, R. January 3, 2016. "Resource Guide to Pricing—Finding Fair Value Exchange." The FairPay Zone. www.fairpayzone.com/p/pricing.html

Rosen, J. 2013. "Why Pierre Omidyar Decided to Join Forces with Glenn Greenwald for a New Venture in News." *PressThink.* http://pressthink.org/2013/10/why-pierre-omidyar-decided-to-join-forces-with-glenn-greenwald-for-a-new-venture-in-news/

Santana, S., and V.G. Morwitz. June 17, 2013. "We're in This Together: How Sellers, Social Values, and Relationship Norms Influence Consumer Payments in Pay-What-You-Want Contexts." Under Revision for Invited Review at *Journal of Marketing.* www8.gsb.columbia.edu/programs-admissions/sites/programs-admissions/files/marketing/seminar_papers/paper_santana_fa13.pdf

Seufert, E.B. 2014. *Freemium Economics: Leveraging Analytics and User Segmentation to Drive Revenue (The Savvy Manager's Guides).* Morgan Kaufmann.

Shapiro, B. July 22, 2002. "Is Performance-Based Pricing the Right Price for You?" Harvard Business School. http://hbswk.hbs.edu/item/is-performance-based-pricing-the-right-price-for-you

Shapiro, C., and H.R. Varian. 1999. *Information Rules: A Strategic Guide to the Network Economy.* Harvard Business Review Press.

Shirky, C. 2000. "The Case Against Micropayments." P2P. www.openp2p.com/lpt/a/515

Smith, A. 1776. *The Wealth of Nations.* Scotland: William Strahan/Thomas Cadell.

Streitfeld, D. 2013. "As New Services Track Habits, the E-Books Are Reading You." *The New York Times,* December 24.

Thaler, R.H., and C.R. Sunstein. 2009. *Nudge.* Penguin.

Thaler, R.H. 2015. "The Power of Nudges, for Good and Bad." *The New York Times,* October 31.

Toffler, A. 1970. *Future Shock.* Random House.

Tzuo, T. December 3, 2012. "Paywall 2.0: Why Focusing on Customers Is the Only Way to Win." *The Guardian.*

Index

OTHER TITLES IN OUR SERVICE SYSTEMS AND INNOVATIONS IN BUSINESS AND SOCIETY COLLECTION

Jim Spohrer, IBM and Haluk Demirkan, Arizona State University, Editors

- *Modeling Service Systems* by Ralph Badinelli
- *Sustainable Service* by Adi Wolfson
- *People, Processes, Services, and Things: Using Services Innovation to Enable the Internet of Everything* by Hazim Dahir, Bil Dry, and Carlos Pignataro
- *Service Design and Delivery: How Design Thinking Can Innovate Business and Add Value to Society* by Toshiaki Kurokawa
- *All Services, All the Time: How Business Services Serve Your Business* by Doug McDavid
- *Obtaining Value from Big Data for Service Delivery* by Stephen H. Kaisler, Frank Armour, and William Money
- *Service Innovation* by Anders Gustafsson, Per Kristensson, Gary R. Schirr, and Lars Witell
- *Matching Services to Markets: The Role of the Human Sensorium in Shaping Service-Intensive Markets* by H.B. Casanova

Announcing the Business Expert Press Digital Library

Concise e-books business students need for classroom and research

This book can also be purchased in an e-book collection by your library as

- a one-time purchase,
- that is owned forever,
- allows for simultaneous readers,
- has no restrictions on printing, and
- can be downloaded as PDFs from within the library community.

Our digital library collections are a great solution to beat the rising cost of textbooks. E-books can be loaded into their course management systems or onto students' e-book readers.
The **Business Expert Press** digital libraries are very affordable, with no obligation to buy in future years. For more information, please visit **www.businessexpertpress.com/librarians**. To set up a trial in the United States, please email **sales@businessexpertpress.com**.

www.ingramcontent.com/pod-product-compliance
Lightning Source LLC
Chambersburg PA
CBHW071632200326
41519CB00012BA/2265